Tcl

VEHICLE BODY REPAIR

Levels 2 and 3

by

ALLAN RENNIE LAE MIMI

Published by:
The Institute of the Motor Industry
Fanshaws
Brickendon
Hertford
SG13 8PQ

© 1997 The Institute of the Motor Industry

ISBN 1 871880 24 6

Publications Manager: Peter Creasey FIMI
Education Manager: Alan Mackrill MBA BEd(Hons) LAE FIMI AssIPD
Series Editor: Harry Darton BSc(Econ)

Designed by: Julian Bennett, Hertford

Originating, printing and binding in Great Britain by:
Black Bear Press Ltd
Kings Hedges Road
Cambridge
CB4 2PQ

THE UNDERPINNING KNOWLEDGE SERIES

Books in the Underpinning Knowledge series, published by The Institute of the Motor Industry, are:

VEHICLE BODY REPAIR
by Allan Rennie LAE MIMI   ISBN 1 871880 24 6

CUSTOMER SERVICE in the Motor Trade
by Bill Naylor FIMI   ISBN 1 871880 39 4

VEHICLE PARTS Administration and Organization
by Tom Colley LAE MIMI   ISBN 1 871880 14 9

VEHICLE MECHANICAL AND ELECTRONIC SYSTEMS
by Andrew Livesey BEd(Hons),IEng,LAE,FIMI   ISBN 1 871880 19 X

VEHICLE FINISHING
by Charles Long MIMI   ISBN 1 871880 29 7

MANAGEMENT Level 3
by Jill Blacklin CertEd,DMS,MBA   ISBN 1 871880 34 3

Enquiries regarding this series and orders for the books should be addressed to:

Publications Manager
The Institute of the Motor Industry
Fanshaws
Brickendon
Hertford
SG13 8PQ
Tel: 01992 511521
Fax: 01992 511548

PUBLISHER'S INTRODUCTION

This book, while giving a general outline of the subject, has been designed primarily to help in the knowledge and understanding required for National Vocational Qualifications (NVQs) in Vehicle Body Repair, Levels 2 and 3.

NVQs are based on national standards required for employment and as such cover all sectors and levels of employment. The assessment of these qualifications is based on a person's ability to show his or her competence against the standards which have been defined. There are no set courses of study or training and the assessment is carried out when the candidate is ready, not when the assessor decrees. There is no pass or failure; the person concerned is either competent or not-yet-competent.

'Competence' means being able to perform the job to the standards expected by employers in the industry. The NVQ is broken down into **Units of Competence**, each of which covers a reasonably self-contained aspect of the occupation. The Units are further sub-divided into **Elements of Competence** and then into **Performance Criteria**. It is against the Performance Criteria with the Range Statements and Knowledge that the candidate is assessed.

While competence is measured in the actual DOING of the task, there is obviously a need for underlying knowledge which the candidate must have in order to be able actually to carry out the practical work involved. This, known in NVQ terms as The Underpinning Knowledge, is the subject matter of this book.

To relate the material here to the part of the NVQ being covered, there are indicators used. The **Unit** is used as the chapter heading and sub-headings indicate the **Elements**. Further sub-division breaks the Elements up into the required **Performance Criteria**, formal setting out of which appears in the text. To assist those who select from the book at the time of familiarising themselves with a *specific* Performance Criteria, the Underpinning Knowledge is detailed in that section, with some information perhaps repeated from other Performance Criteria, or a cross-reference is given to the related section or sections.

The Institute of the Motor Industry, publisher of this series of books, is the major awarding body for NVQs in the motor industry. We wish all our readers following the NVQ trail great success in their careers and hope that this information will bolster their abilities to perform their jobs to the best possible levels of competence and to their greatest satisfaction.

It is, however, our hope that readers will not see the NVQ as the end of the qualification trail, but rather the beginning. On successful completion of your NVQ programme, we look forward to welcoming you into membership of the Institute of the Motor Industry. Our letters after your name will identify you to the world in general as a dedicated professional, will serve as witness to your total competence and your full commitment to your industry and your career.

ROY WARD FIMI
Director General
The Institute of the Motor Industry

Author's Preface

WE ARE ALL PART OF THIS INNOVATIVE - AND RESPONSIBLE - INDUSTRY

This book will give you the underpinning knowledge that you require for the job that you do or hope to do. This is an exciting industry, where technology is marching on apace; there are always great new developments, emphasising the need for you to keep right up to date with what is happening in your part of the motor business.

But we also live in the wider context of the community as a whole and it is always necessary to take account of our great responsibility as part of an industry that impinges on the wider welfare of all, arguably more so than any other.

This is an area in which the organisation in which I work myself, Kilmarnock College in Scotland, is making its contribution. I will detail, for example, one important current project.

The proliferation of plastic products has led to problems, both environmental and economic. Because of the relative economic benefits, damaged plastic products have been simply thrown away. As most plastics are non bio-degradable, the only practical disposal has been through ever-decreasing land-fill sites. In addition, the replacement of these discarded products puts pressure on scarce, and expensive, non-renewable fossil-fuel sources with all the accompanying pollution associated with petro-chemical production processes. The industry is now being forced to reassess past practices because of recent Environmental Protection Acts as well as the economic squeeze on margins.

Fifty percent of all plastic products are repairable cost-effectively and Kilmarnock College is helping to develop the skills necessary for the repair and re-use of products such as car bumpers, head-lamp casings and so on.

As the use of plastics across the industrial environment increases, so will the economic and environmental imperative for greener and more cost-effective practices become greater. As one indicator, we are now receiving endorsements from some of the major insurance companies, who see the benefits of plastic repair as a major beneficial alternative to wasteful throw-away practices.

So I hope you will see the industry from this perspective - to employ our complex technical skills against a background of the needs of the community at large, to recognise the imperative to set the undoubted advantages of the motor vehicle against the need for a better and better environment.

Allan Rennie LAE MIMI

ACKNOWLEDGEMENTS

The publishers and author gratefully acknowledge the immense contribution made by the following companies who gave permission for the reproduction of illustrations: Sykes Pickavant; Protoplas; Autodata; Blackhawk; Ford Motor Company; JOSAM; Car-O-Liner; Car Bench International.

Acknowledgement is also due to Julie McHoul whose patience and hard work in the initial compiling of this book is very much appreciated.

Contents

REPLACE VEHICLE BODY PANELS, PANEL SECTIONS AND ANCILLARY FITTINGS

A2.1   REMOVE BODY PANELS, PANEL SECTIONS AND ANCILLARY FITTINGS TO ALLOW REPAIR/REPLACEMENT

A2.1.1   Appropriate information is accessed from appropriate sources to inform the required removal activities

Before any removal activities take place you will have to acquaint yourself with the information required to perform the removal operation without causing any unnecessary damage.

Reference can be made to the types of publications listed below:
- Manufacturer's Workshop Manuals
- Repair Schedules as published by organisations such as *Thatchams Insurance Repair And Research Centre.*
- *Autodata Books*

These listed publications will inform you of the sequence of panel removal and where and what types of fasteners are used. To ascertain the panels, panel sections and ancillary fittings that require to be removed during the repair process, refer to the estimate and job card which will give full details.

If you cannot find the information required, or you are working on an unfamiliar vehicle, ask your supervisor for help. This person, or some of your colleagues, may have worked on this type of vehicle in the past.

A2.1.2   Protective clothing and equipment appropriate to the removal activities are used

As with all workshop activities, you are required to wear and use all the necessary safety clothing and equipment, not only to protect yourself and your colleagues, but also the vehicle you are working on, from any unnecessary damage.

Protective clothing and equipment fall into two main categories:

1. **Operator Protection**

   Gloves

   Rubber for protection against chemicals, sealers and solvents;

Leather for protection against welding rays, hot metal and sharp edges of sheet metal.

Apron

Rubber for protection against chemicals, sealers and solvents;

Leather for protection against welding rays and sparks.

Overalls

These should always be worn in the workshop for general protection against dirt, dust, oil and grease. When carrying out welding operations, overalls made from flame-retardent material should be worn. Overalls made from nylon material should not be worn in a motor vehicle workshop.

Footwear

Safety footwear should always be worn to protect your feet from the hazards of vehicles running over them or heavy objects falling on them.

All safety footwear will have steel toe-caps fitted. Boots that have the steel toe-caps fitted to the outside of the boot should not be worn in the paint shop due to the risk of sparks.

Goggles

Clear goggles should be worn when sanding, grinding, drilling and any other form of material removal. Tinted and shaded goggles and face shield should be worn when welding or flame cutting. It is important to note that goggles used for oxy-acetylene welding will not give adequate protection against ultra-violet rays produced when MAGS, TAGS and MMA welding.

Respiratory

Various grades of face mask are available, depending on the type of job being carried out. One of the greatest hazards associated with body repair is that from dust particles. Under the COSHH regulations it is essential that respiratory protection should be worn. Make yourself familiar with the various types of face mask available and the situation where each would be worn.

Ventilation/dust extraction

There should be suitable ventilation to remove fumes from welding and vapours from sealers and adhesives, especially when using heat to remove sealers or sound/anti-drum pads, and to extract dust particles produced when grinding or sanding. Ventilation and dust extraction may be portable or be a fixed system. This will normally be governed by the size of workshop and the number of persons employed.

2. Vehicle Protection

Dust Covers

Used to protect the seats and interior trim from contamination from dirt, dust and grease that may be present in the workshop. These covers are usually made from lightweight polythene or paper.

Anti-Spark Covers

To be placed over the vehicle glass and adjacent panels to protect against damage from sparks when grinding and welding.

Fire extinguishers

A suitable fire extinguisher should always be at hand when heating, welding or flame cutting. A list of the type and application for fire extinguishers can be found in element *A13.2.6.*

A2.1.3 *Components, ancillary fittings and, where appropriate, surface treatments are removed using approved methods and equipment*

Panels and part panels can be removed for two reasons: first, because they are damaged; or, second, to allow access to other damaged areas. Panels that have sustained damage are normally replaced. Panels fall into two groups :

i. **Stressed panels** which are welded in position and form an integral part of the vehicle body-shell or the cab of a commercial vehicle.
ii. **Non-stressed panels.** These panels are either bolted, screwed or riveted into position; some may even be held in position by special adhesives. This type of panel - wings, doors, boot/tailgate and bonnets - do not normally contribute to the strength of the body shell, but may be designed to assist in the protection of the vehicle occupants.

In order to carry out any repair or replacement to damaged panels it may be necessary to remove some of the ancillary fittings that are attached to or in close proximity to the panels being replaced. Examples of these ancillary fittings would be internal and external trim, lights, windows, window regulator and some minor mechanical components. These items will be listed on the estimate or job card under MET (Mechanical,

Electrical and Trim). In order to stay within the time allocated for the job, you should not remove items of MET that do not affect the repair, while still removing enough to allow the repair/replacement to be carried out without causing any damage.

When removing items of trim you should familiarise yourself with the type of fasteners being used. On many items of trim, both internal and external, the fastening devices are not visible, so if force is used some of the plastic clips, studs or even the trim itself may be unnecessarily damaged. If some items are difficult to remove, check with your supervisor or consult one of the sources of information listed in *A2.1.1.*

Always use the correct tool for the job being done. You should familiarise yourself with all the common screw, stud and bolt heads being used; for example, many foreign-manufactured vehicles have Torx-headed screws. Never use a Philips screwdriver on a Pozidrive screw. Security screws are becoming more common, so a good quality security bit set should be used. These sets have a selection of bits to remove all the common security fasteners used.

Glass may have to be removed, either because it is broken or to aid panel replacement. Extra care should be taken with glass because of the ease with which it may break or chip. Front and rear screen windows can be held in place by one of two methods:

i **Bonded** (direct glazed)

This type of window is held in place by a high-density exceptionally strong adhesive. This adhesive has to be cut to remove the window, this can be done using a special pneumatic knife or cheese type wire. They are replaced using new sealer which must be allowed to cure fully before returning the vehicle to service. This type of window is normally of laminated construction.

Direct glazed windows offer many advantages:

- an increase in body rigidity due to the glass being integrated on to the body.
- a better seal against water ingress.
- improved safety feature due to the glass, which is laminated, remaining intact should the occupants be propelled towards it.

ii **Rubber Gasket** (indirect glazed)

With this type, the rubber gasket is lipped over a flange on the windscreen arpeture. Some are self-sealing and some may require the use of a mastic sealer. Indirect glazed windows do not offer the same strengths and safety characters as that of direct glazed windows.

When removing door drop-glass windows, side or quarter-light windows, care should be taken not to damage or chip the windows on the edges as they may shatter. This is due to the fact that all side windows are of toughened glass.

Where windows cannot be removed to facilitate a repair, they should be adequately covered to prevent damage from grinding spark, or from welding spatter, which is very difficult, if not impossible, to remove.

When removing any items of electrical equipment - such as front and rear lights, horn, door or trim-mounted speakers, rear wiper motors and electrical components fitted to doors (such as central locking or electrically operated windows) - you will have to disconnect the wire connections. Normally, these electrical connections are made with the use of a multi-plug which will only fit one way. This eliminates the possibility of reconnecting the electrical components the wrong way, which could cause damage to the units.

Should the electrical components be wired with the use of individual terminals, it may be necessary to tape each wire and write on the tape where the individual wires are located. This is even more important should there be a large time lapse between stripping down and reassembling.

Some wires may have to be cut and rejoined at a later date. These are best reconnected using a soldering joint rather than a mechanical fastener such as a scotch-lock connector. Soldered joints are more permanent and offer excellent resistance to failure should they be exposed to the elements.

The removal of external scuff mouldings, badges and coach lines will be eased with the use of a heat gun and the gentle application of heat to loosen the adhesive. Any adhesive remaining on the panel surface may be removed using a weak solvent cleaner.

Panel sealers and sound-deadening pads can also be removed with the use of gentle heat and a scraper. An oxy-acetylene flame should not be used, as dangerous fumes may be given off should the sealing materials be burnt or heated to too high a temperature.

After the removal of all the necessary ancillary fittings, the removal of the damaged panels can begin.

As previously mentioned, panels or part panels are removed for two reasons: to facilitate a repair or because the panel itself is damaged. The removal procedure differs for the two types of panel fitted - non-stressed or stressed.

Non-stressed panel removal

Non-stressed panels do not form an integral part of the body-shell strength but do contribute to the protection of the occupants in the vehicle. Typical examples of non-stressed panels include bolt-on front wings, bonnet, doors, boot lid and tail gate. Although these panels are non-stressed, many vehicles incorporate side-impact bars such as those used by Volvo's SIPS (Side Impact Protection System), which not only protect against side impacts but also restrain the interior from collapse during a head-on collision.

The removal of these non-stressed panels is straight-forward, they may be bolted, screwed or riveted to the vehicle body.

Wings

When removing wings, especially on vehicles with which you are unfamiliar, first ensure you know the location of all the bolts and screws holding them in place. This information may be obtained from the data described in *2.1.1*. Alternatively, where a new wing is being fitted, a close look at the new wing will establish the location points. After all the screws and bolts have been removed, it may be necessary to loosen the sealer bonding the wing along its joints with the vehicle. This may be done with the use of a hot-air gun and a sharp scraper or knife. After the wing has been removed, any damaged sealer should be completely removed prior to fitting and alignment of the new wing.

Doors

Doors are attached to the vehicle by one of two methods - bolted hinges or welded hinges.

Bolted Hinges

These hinges are normally bolted to the vehicle door and on to the vehicle pillar ('A' post at the front; 'C' post at the rear). When removing the door, it is advisable to get support and take up the weight as the door is removed. If there is no damage to the hinges or the pillars, remove the bolts from the hinge attached to the door and not the pillar; if there is damage to the hinges or the pillars, the door may be removed complete with hinges. Start by removing all but one bolt from each hinge, leaving the last bolt until the door is ready to be lifted away. Special support frames are available to hold the door during removal or refitting, which eliminates the need for two people to carry out the job.

6

Welded Hinges

With this type of hinge, one part is welded to the pillar and the other part is welded to the door frame. Removal is carried out by extracting the hinge pin with the use of a special hinge-pin removal tool. On occasion, the hinge pin may seize inside the hinge. If this does occur, it may be necessary to apply heat to the hinge, which will cause the hinge rivet to expand and allow the pin to be drawn out. If this is not successful, it may be necessary to cut through the pin at the hinge joints using a fine hacksaw blade and then drilling out the old hinge pin.

A door hinge pin remover/replacer

Bonnet, Boot and Tailgate

These are removed by unbolting the hinges from the panels or vehicle body, whichever is the most convenient or accessible. This is normally a two-man job and extreme care must be taken not to cause any damage to the body or panel being removed.

Stressed panels

Stressed panels are attached to the bodyshell using various welding techniques, the most common being resistance spot, although some joints may be MAGS or resistance-seam welded. These panels form an integral part of the bodyshell and contribute to giving the body its maximum structural rigidity. They must therefore be repaired or replaced in accordance with the vehicle manufacturer's specification.

Stressed panel removal

Various methods may be adopted for the removal of stressed panels - by the use of a pneumatic chisel, by plasma cutting, by power saw, or by grinding and drilling. Ideally, the method used should reflect the accessibility, size and type of panel to be removed and the replacement procedure adopted. As a rough guide, it would be advisable to select the removal operation that will allow the panel to be removed with the least number of cuts and will offer the minimum amount of distortion or damage to the flanges or supports that hold the panel in its correct alignment. The use of pneumatic chisels is not so widely accepted for panel removal, due to their high noise output and their failure to allow cutting accurately without the need for further flange spot-weld removal.

For panels that have spot-welded joints that are lapped together, the spot welds should first be drilled out and the panels carefully separated, using a hammer and a fine wide-bladed chisel.

To determine the location of the spot welds, the joint areas should be cleaned to remove paint, sealer etc that may be covering the spot-weld nugget. The use of a small belt sander, hot-air gun, oxy-acetylene flame and wire brush will help in preparing the joint edges before spot-weld removal begins. Spot welds can be removed firstly by centre dabbing each weld nugget then drilling through the outer skin only, using a suitable size drill, or alternatively with the use of a Zipcut tool which drills the outer panel with a saw-like bit, thus releasing the area around the spot weld.

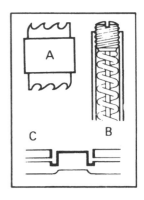

Zipcut spot-weld remover

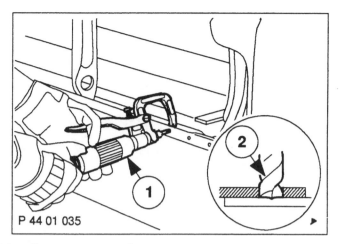

Spot-weld milling cutting tool

For extensively damaged areas, where the use of a drill is not possible until the damaged panel has been removed, rough cutting can be carried out using the pneumatic chisel, hacksaw, snips or shears; or it may be burned off using an oxy-acetylene cutting flame; or with the use of a plasma cutter. Before any hot cutting is carried out, thoroughly check all around the area to be cut to ensure there are no flammable materials that could be ignited by any stray sparks or flames, and before plasma cutting ensure the battery has been disconnected. A small cutting disk attached to a grinderette may be used to remove any areas of a panel that may have been MAGS welded, also for the removal of the weld nugget from the flanges of the undamaged areas after the damaged panels have been removed.

Where only a part panel has to be removed, the damaged panel may be cut using a fine-blade hacksaw, after being carefully marked. This will allow a clean even edge ready to receive the new panel for welding. After all the damaged panels have been removed and all the misalignment rectified, the attachment areas and flanges must be carefully dressed and prepared before any panel or part-panel replacement begins.

A2.1.4 *Components, ancillary fittings and, where appropriate, surface treatments are removed in accordance with the work specification for the vehicle*

The removal of all the components and ancillary fittings must tie in with what has been described on the work schedule or job card. The job

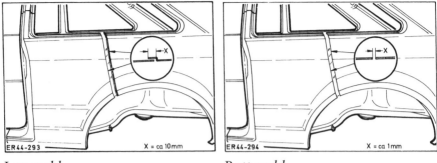

Lap-weld   *Butt-weld*

card will have been prepared using information detailed on the estimate, so it is most important that you adhere to the instructions listed.

A2.1.5 Removal activities minimise the risk of damage to surrounding body areas

It is wise to adopt a planned and methodical approach to the removal activity, which will help minimise any damage to the areas surrounding the damage. For example, if you try to force off a panel which is still held by a fastener or weld that you have not seen, you may fracture, dent or rip the part of body that was previously undamaged. This will result in unnecessary time-consuming rectification work, for which your company is unable to claim payment for your time. If you find yourself in any doubt, always ask for assistance, or consult the data previously described in *2.1.1*.

A2.1.6 Where there is potential disturbance to electrical, mechanical, electronic or other systems, appropriate authorised assistance is sought if required

You may find that, during the stripping down of a vehicle to facilitate a repair, many sophisticated items of electrical, electronic or mechanical compartments may have to be removed. This is more likely when you are repairing a vehicle which has sustained damage to the front end, including suspension, steering and damage within the engine bay. If you require the removal of any component that you have no knowledge of, it is advisable to request assistance from a specialist in these systems. A motor mechanic may be required to assist in the removal of the mechanical items such as suspension and steering and damaged components on an engine or gear box. This is even more important if the items that have to be removed require special restraints put in place until they are replaced or if they will require readjustment and setting on reassemble. Many modern motor vehicles, both private and commercial, are fitted with complex and intricate electronic engine management systems, fuel injection (EFI) and anti-lock brakes (ABS). The services of an auto electrician will be required, as this specialism is outside the scope of work carried out by a body-repair technician.

A2.1.7   Removal activities are completed within approved timescales

In the case of repair to a damaged vehicle, time will have been carefully estimated and allocated to each operation - removal, replacement/repair, painting and reassembling. In order that a reasonable profit is made from a repair job, the time schedule for each operation must be closely adhered to. Spending too much time on one part of the repair schedule will have two drawbacks. Firstly, it may not allow sufficient time for the following stages, which may result in corners being cut, thus turning out an inferior repair; or, secondly, this could result in the job being worked on during time that cannot be claimed for against the estimate. This could have a knock-on effect in that it could be taking time you could be spending on another job.

A2.1.8   Where removal activities are likely to exceed the approved time scale, the circumstances are reported promptly to an authorised person

For some reasons, which may be outside your control, you may not be able to carry out the job you are doing in the allocated time scale. If you discover you are in this situation, you should report this immediately to your supervisor. A typical example of the need for extra time on the job would be the discovery of hidden damage not only on the body but also mechanical or electrical, which may require extra time during the stripping-down process to allow greater access to facilitate the repair. If this occurs and it is reported promptly, it gives your supervisor time to apply to the customer, who may be the vehicle owner, or the insurance company, who is paying the final bill. The customer may want to come into the workshop and view the extent of the extra work required; alternatively a supplementary estimate may have to be generated and permission to continue granted. This is more important if the vehicle is a border-line case during the original analysis, where the damage may have rendered the vehicle a 'write off'.

*A2.1.9   Removal activities are performed in accordance with statutory
and organisational policy and procedures for health and
safety*

The company where you are employed will have rules laid down which
control the way you conduct yourself in the workshop. These will cover
areas such as :

- The way in which you conduct yourself with regards to health and
  safety; your compliance with the COSHH and EPA regulations.
- Your attitude and respect for your colleagues.
- The method you go about your work.

Your employer has a responsibility under the Health and Safety at
Work Act and the COSHH regulations, to look after your health and
ensure that you know how to carry out the work safely. Therefore it is
essential that you follow these rules, as you could be subject to
disciplinary action should you disregard them.

If you follow the guidelines laid down in *A2.1.2* you will be going a
long way towards working in an efficient and safe manner.

A2.2 POSITION AND FIX REPLACEMENT BODY PANELS, PANEL SECTIONS AND ANCILLARY FITTINGS

A2.2.1 Appropriate information is accessed from appropriate sources to inform the fitting of replacement components and ancillary fittings

Refer to *A2.1.1* for general information on data. For specific dimensions on panel alignment, reference points can be taken from adjacent panels that remained intact and undamaged.

A2.2.2 Protective clothing and equipment appropriate to the replacement activities are used

Refer to *A2.1.2*.

A2.2.3 Replacement components and ancillary fittings meet specifications for dimensions, materials and functional capability

When replacement components and fittings are being selected during a repair operation, either mechanical or body, these parts must be able to serve the function for which they were selected. Components and fittings can be obtained from two sources:

i   **From the vehicle manufacturer's dealer network, through a local dealer.** These parts will be genuine manufacturer's parts and will therefore be covered by the manufacturer's warranty. This will allow the vehicle to be repaired and returned to service in pre-accident condition. It is advisable that OE (original equipment) parts should be used if a vehicle is still under the manufacturer's warranty.

ii **Specialist body and mechanical parts manufacturers.** These parts are produced for the older car, where the manufacturer's warranty no longer applies. The quality of these parts may be every bit as good as OE parts but are not fully recognised as replacement for genuine parts.

Whichever source the replacements are obtained from, it is important that they meet all the dimensional and functional capabilities expected from them.

A2.2.4 Positioning of replacement components and ancillary fittings conforms to vehicle specifications

When fitting replacement parts they must be adjusted and positioned in accordance with the vehicle manufacturer's specifications. Details of body dimensions can be obtained from *Autodata* books or *Thatcham* repair manuals. Many of the dimensions for body panels are taken from adjacent panels that have not been removed or damaged. Bolt-on panels, such as boot lid, bonnet and doors, are gapped and adjusted using the naked eye as a guide. These panels usually have some degree of adjustment to allow for any alterations required.

Positioning and adjustment of mechanical components differ from those of body panels in that their adjustments normally have specific measurements - for example, fan belts, timing belts etc. will have a set tension requirement to allow them to function satisfactorily. All steering and suspension items are adjusted to very small tolerances. Failure to adjust and set-up steering and suspension components to the manufacturer's specification can affect the handling characteristics of the vehicle and may also render the vehicle unroadworthy. Steering misalignment may cause excessive premature tyre wear and also cause uneven braking.

Details of mechanical adjustments can be available from the many data books published or from the specific vehicle workshop manual.

Note: If you are in any doubt about fitting and adjusting mechanical or electrical components, inform your supervisor or call on the services of someone who is trained in the specific area with which you are unfamiliar.

Incorrect fitting and adjustment of mechanical and electrical items can lead to extremely expensive rectification repairs at a later date.

A2.2.5 Components and ancillary fittings are refitted using approved methods, materials and equipment

When refitting components and ancillary fittings, they should be replaced exactly as they were before they were removed and should be held in place using the same method that was used during manufacture.

The refitting of components - that is, body panels - falls into two main categories:
   a) Stressed panels, which will normally be welded on, and
   b) Non-stressed panels, which are normally held in position by bolts, screws or adhesives.

We will start by first looking at the refitting of stressed panels as many of the non-stressed panels are fitted to the stressed panels. Panels such as doors, boot-lid, bonnet and bolt-on wings should be made available to aid in the realignment of the panels being welded in place which form an integral part of the body shell or commercial vehicle cab.

STRESSED PANEL FITTING. Before offering up a new panel, ensure that all the flanges, both on the vehicle and the panel, are suitably dressed and free from any damage or twists. With this done, offer up the new panel to the vehicle and ensure it touches all around its mounting points. If it is difficult to fit at any one area, never use excessive force as there may still be some trimming or grinding of edges required. When all trimming has been carried out, offer up the panel again. It can be held in place by the use of mole/vice grips and, where grips cannot be fitted, the temporary use of self-tapping screws may be a suitable alternative. When you are satisfied that the panel is going to fit, remove it once more and apply a weld-through primer to all the edges that are to be welded.

Note. Take care when using this primer. Wear a suitable mask if applying using an aerosol can. Also use suitable ventilation when welding, as these weld-through primers contain zinc-oxide which will release dangerous fumes when heated.

Finally refit the new panel. Align and clamp the panel into position. Check the alignment against adjacent panels. It may be necessary temporarily to rehang a door, boot or bonnet to check alignment. It may also be necessary temporarily to refit a radiator grille, front or tail lamp or bumper to aid in final adjustment or alignment of the new panel.

When you are satisfied the new panel is fitted and aligned correctly you can start to weld it in place. If using a resistance spot-welder, always carry out a test weld on scrap metal similar to that of which the vehicle in made. This is extremely important, as the welder settings vary, depending on the thickness of the metals being joined. When the spot-welder is finally set, stagger your weld around the panel. Never start at one edge and continue around back to the point where you started, as this may cause unnecessary distortion.

The spot-welds on any one flange should equal in number and pitch to those of the vehicle manufacturer, or those laid down in the repair manual. Any area which cannot be spot-welded may be plug-welded, using the MAGS welding process. Many of the repair manuals outline the type of welds to use.

Checking wing clearance with adjacent panels

Where a panel butts against another panel, this joint should be tacked and welded using the MAGS welding process. To minimise distortion on a butt-welded joint, use plenty of tack welds close together and ensure an even gap is maintained along the joint. The width of the gap should be about the thickness of a hacksaw blade.

After the panel has been welded in place, any plug or seam welds should be ground or sanded down in preparation for filling or priming.

NON-STRESSED PANEL FITTINGS. Typical non-stressed panels that are commonly replaced, due to accident damage or corrosion damage repair, are bolt-on wings, doors, boot and bonnets. These may be fitted as a single panel or a combination of panels.

Replacement panel clamped ready for welding

Spot-weld operation around flanges

MAGS welding along part panel joints

Doors. When fitting new doors or re-hanging doors that have been removed, first remove the striker plate from the closing pillar. This will ensure the door will not jam shut if it is not in correct alignment. Once the door has been fitted it should be adjusted to ensure that there is an even gap all round and that any swage lines or mouldings align with adjacent panels. Doors are held in position by one of two methods - either bolted on hinges, or by means of removable hinge pins. With bolted hinges, adjustment can be made up or down, in or out, back and forward. This type of door, although offering excellent adjustment positions, is generally more difficult to align. Doors which are held with removable hinge pins do not offer any adjustment. Minor adjustment can be made using force, with the aid of wooden blocks placed as supports and the opposite edge of the door being pushed into position. Once you are satisfied that the door is in correct alignment, refit the striker plate. Do not over-tighten until the door closes without hitting the striker plate, which may cause the door to lift or be pushed down when closed. The door should also close fully on the second catch without excessive slamming.

When fitting a combination of panels, for example, a door and a wing or two doors and wing, always fit and adjust the doors to suit the body; then fit the wing and align to suit the door and bonnet or boot.

Wings. When fitting wings ensure they have been sealed and the underside treated with the recommended anti-rust treatment. It is advisable to paint all areas that cannot be painted once the wing is fitted. As with fitting a door, the wing should have an even gap along the edge of the bonnet and down the edge of the door. If the gap down the door edge is too wide this may result in the front edge of the wing protruding further than the front of the bonnet, thus making the bonnet difficult to align. Ensure that swage lines and mouldings also align with the adjacent panels.

If an aerial has been fitted, it will be advisable to drill the hole before the wing is fitted, since it may be difficult to drill at a later stage or may cause damage to the paintwork after refinishing. Check that lights and indicators also align with the new wing before final tightening.

Boot-lid, tail gates, bonnet. The method of fitting these panels is similar to that of fitting doors. It may be necessary to have an extra pair of hands available as these panels can be larger and heavier than a door. When fitting these panels the gap has not only to be even down the edge but also equal on both sides.

BONDED AND SEALED PANELS. Bonding is used by some manufacturers to hold strengthening frames to the inside of a boot or bonnet. It may also be used to hold a door skin on to the door frame. This joining method will give added water leak and corrosion protection, as well as giving extra strength at certain joints.

These adhesives should be applied in accordance with the manufacturer's recommendations.

All health and safety rules must be observed, but as a guide-line always wear rubber gloves, overalls and goggles and use in a well ventilated area and observe the NO SMOKING rule when in use.

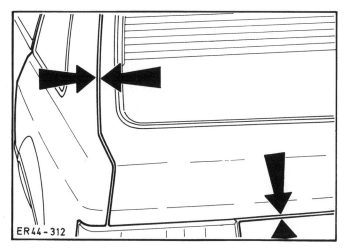

Check gap all round tail gate

ANCILLARY FITTINGS. The ancillary fittings, such as internal and external trim, front and rear lights and windows, are normally fitted after the vehicle has been refinished. Great care should be taken to ensure they are fitted in accordance with the manufacturer's recommendations.

Items such as exterior mouldings and name badges are commonly held in place using a double-sided adhesive tape. When refitting these items you only have one try, so it is up to you to ensure that they are in the exact position and correctly aligned before pressing into place. It is good practice to make a mark, using either masking tape or a chalk line, as a guide to their exact position. Once these items are stuck firmly in place you may cause unnecessary damage should you have to remove them for realignment, especially if the vehicle has recently been removed from an oven after painting, when the paint may be dry but not fully hard. Any items of trim that are held in position using either pop rivets or self-tapping screws should be fitted using the same type of screw as the original - the appearance of an item may be spoiled if one screw is a slotted head screw and the rest either Phillips or pozidrive head screw. Similarly, when tightening up screws, use the correct tool. A Phillips screwdriver may cause damage to a pozidrive screw and vice versa. Nuts and bolts should be tightened up using the correct spanner or socket. Some sizes of spanner and socket are similar between AF and metric, which is all right when lightly tightening components. But if these components have to be tightened to a specific high torque, use the exact size required to avoid rounding or damaging the bolt or nut.

19

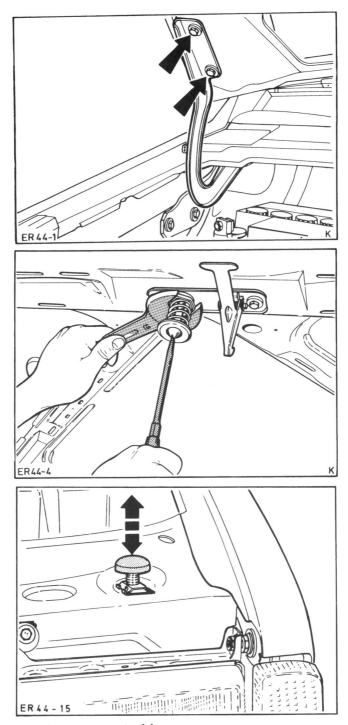

Adjustment points on a typical bonnet

When fitting internal trim items - for example, roof cloth, seats, dash boards and door trims - always wear clean overalls and ensure your hands are clean. This will avoid unnecessary oily or dirty fingermarks or dirt from your overalls marking the upholstery. It is good practice to fit plastic disposable seat covers and paper floor mats as an aid to protection.

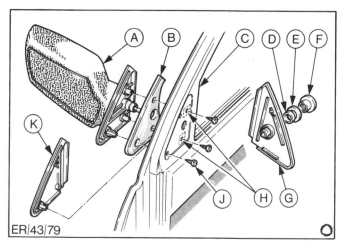

Example of a door-mirror assembly

A - Remote mirror assembly. B - Pad. C - Caulking compound. D - Cloth tape. E - Washer. F - Retaining nut. G - Inner cover. H - Tape. J - Retaining screws. K - Blanking cover.

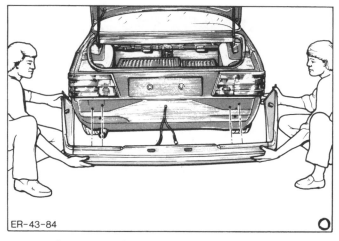

Installing a rear bumper. Always get assistance to prevent unnecessary damage

WINDOW FITTINGS. The fixed windows of a motor vehicle - such as the windscreen, the rear and some side windows - are of two types. They are either bonded to the window aperture or held in place using a rubber gasket, details of which were given in *A2.1.3*.

A typical method of refitting an **indirect** glazed window is:
- clean the window channel in the rubber gasket to ensure there is no trace of sealer or broken glass.
- if it is a gasket that requires a sealing compound, place a small bead all round the gasket in the window channel.
- Fit the rubber gasket on to the window, ensuring it is the correct way round and seated all the way round.
- Lay the window flat on a suitably covered bench with the inside of the window pointing upwards.
- Position the pull cords into the body flange channel of the rubber gasket - these cords are used to pull the rubber lip over the body flange. The pull cord should be overlapped at the bottom of the window by approximately 300 mm (12").
- Using an assistant, carefully lift the window and place into its aperture, placing the two ends of the pull cord inside the vehicle. Move the window into its correct position.
- With one person inside the vehicle pulling the cords and the other outside applying light pressure, start pulling the cord in an upward direction and at an angle in the direction in which you require to travel around the screen.
- Once the lip has been pulled over the flange at the start, proceed around the first corner, after which the other end may be pulled around the other lower corner. Then gradually work with each cord until the rubber lip is fully over the body flange.
- The window can now be settled into position using gentle blows with a rubber mallet around the outside of the rubber.
- Any chrome or plastic trim may now be fitted to the rubber.
- The window should now be cleaned inside and outside and tested for water leaks.

Variation to this method may be required dependent on the make and model being repaired. The repair manual will give exact details of window replacement.

Direct glazed windows may be fitted as set out below - as a guideline only, since fitting methods may vary from one manufacturer to another.

- Trim off any sealer that remains around the window aperture - and round the window, if you are refitting the original windscreen.
- Thoroughly clean both the aperture and the inner side of the window, using a suitable solvent.
- Fit any required spacer blocks in the correct position around the window aperture.

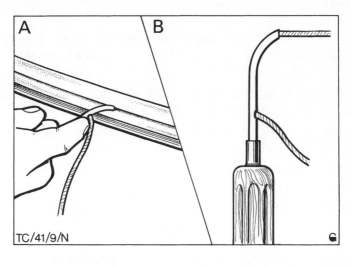

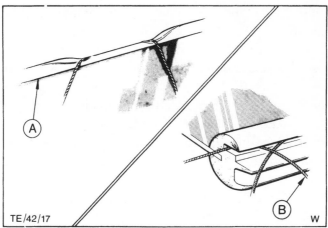

Fitting indirect glazed windows. Top diagram: A - Insertion of tool in weatherstrip groove; B - Tool for insertion of drawcord into weatherstrip groove. Bottom diagram: A - Typical method of lipping weatherstrip over aperture flange using drawcord pulled towards centre of glass; B - Crossing over of drawcord ends.

- Using suitably positioned suction cups, locate the window into the aperture and centralise. When you are sure the window is in its correct position, mark a line from the edge of the window and on to the vehicle body at several positions around its perimeter. The use of masking tape or chalk is required for this operation. This will assist in the correct window location once final fitting takes place.
- Apply an even coat of glass primer to the window and the aperture. Allow to dry, then wipe with a cloth.
- Using a suitable sealer, apply in a smooth continuous bead around the edge of the windscreen. The dimensions of the bead of sealer should be 12mm (0.5 ") in height and approximately 7mm (0.25") wide at the base. **Note:** Before using the sealer, read the instructions on the cartridge and follow them to the letter.
- Using the suction cups, lift the windscreen and offer it up to the vehicle. Carefully align the previously-applied masking tape or chalk-mark guide lines and lower the screen into position. Remove the suction cups.
- The windscreen can now be tested for leaks. If a leak is found, do not attempt to remove the screen; simply apply more sealer to the leak area and re-test.
- The windscreen finishing trim can now be refitted, taking care not to put too much pressure on the window - it may move, as the sealer is not cured.

Important point to note: Until the sealer has fully cured (as indicated on the cartridge), the doors should not be slammed shut with their windows fully closed.

Much of the upper body strength, and of the safety of the vehicle occupants, is dependant on the bonded windscreen being fitted in accordance with the manufacturer's recommendations. It is, therefore, imperative that you follow all instructions fully and precisely.

REFITTING COMPONENTS TO DOOR SHELL

When fitting up a door shell this should be done in reverse order to the way in which it was dismantled. A suggested procedure would be:
- Carefully slide door drop glass into inner shell of door.
- Fit rubber seal around inside of door window frame.
- Push window up into frame into its closed position and jam in place.
- Fit side slide channels to inside of door.

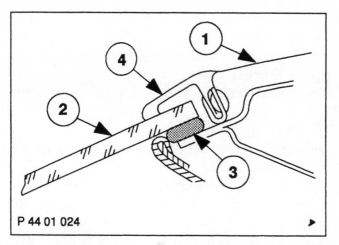

Cross-section of a direct glazed window. 1 - Window frame; 2 - Window glass; 3 - Adhesive; 4 - Cover strip or rubber.

- Fit window regulator to lower slides on the window and adjust until the retaining bolt holes line up with the door frame. Bolt into position and test window operation.
- Fit exterior door handle, lock and door catch.
- Fit interior door handle and test that the door can be opened and closed from both inside and outside the vehicle. Don't forget to test the locking system as well.

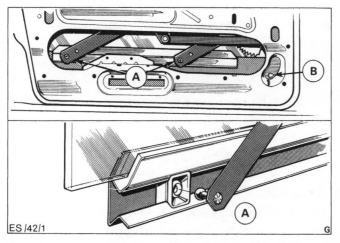

Example of a window regulator mounting points and channel connections. A - Window channel to regulator connectors; B - Door glass run extension securing screw.

- Fit the inner rain plastic sheet (shower curtain) and seal all around its edge.
- The interior panel, the door and window handles and the arm rests can now be fitted.

Finally, re-test all operations of the door and adjust as required.

FRONT AND REAR LIGHTS

Front Lights. When fitting front lights, it is a good practice to lay a large piece of soft material on the floor in front of the vehicle and lay the lamp face down. Locate all the wires to be connected and ensure all screws and clips are at hand. Fit new bulbs as required to the headlamp. Place headlamp into position on front holding panel and screw into position. Do not let go of the lamp until you are sure it is firmly held in place. Connect the wires and test all lights for correct operation; that is, full beam, dipped beam, side light and indicator. After the headlamp has been fitted, the beam alignment must be checked and adjusted. Correct headlamp alignment is a compulsory item of the annual MOT test.

Rear Light Cluster. As with the head lamp, care should be taken not to cause any damage during fitting. The fitting procedure is similar to that of the front lamp, the main difference being that the rear lamps are fitted with a rubber water seal/gasket because they protrude within the boot area and no water should be allowed to enter past the lamp. After fitting, test for correct operation and also check for any water leaks.

A2.2.6 *Sealants are selected and applied according to manufacturers'*
specification for type, method of application and thickness

Before any sealant materials are used, you must familiarise yourself with all necessary safety precautions and equipment. Many sealants give off toxic vapours and if they come into contact with the skin they are very difficult to remove.

When selecting a suitable sealer, it is wise first to consult the repair manual to determine what type of sealer was used during manufacture. Some vehicle manufacturers supply the sealers as an OE part, although specialist companies, such as 3M, Tereson and Sikaflex, will produce a sealer that will match that of the sealer applied during original vehicle assembly.

When applying the sealer to panel joints or edges, the finished look and texture must match that of the original.

A2.2.7   Where there is potential disturbance to electrical, mechanical,
*   electronic or other systems, appropriate authorised assistance*
*   is sought if required*

It is most important, when reassembling a vehicle after repair, that you do not attempt to fit, connect or adjust any item of mechanical, electrical or electronic systems with which you are unfamiliar. An incorrectly fitted or adjusted timing belt may either slip or break, causing extensive internal damage to an engine. Incorrectly aligned and adjusted steering, suspension or brakes will not only cause uneven tyre wear but may impair the handling characteristics of the vehicle, even rendering it unroadworthy. Electrical or electronic equipment may be polarity sensitive - that is, dependent on whether the system applies positive or negative earth - and, if connected up incorrectly, may cause the equipment unnecessary damage, to the extent that short circuit or even vehicle fire may occur.

It is for these reasons that you must seek authorised assistance from a specialist during the reassembly.

A2.2.8   Replacement activities are completed within the approved
*   timescales*

Refer to *A2.1.7.*

A2.2.9   Where replacement activities are likely to exceed the approved
*   timescale, the circumstances are reported promptly to an*
*   authorised person*

If, during reassembly of a vehicle, you discover you cannot complete the job within the time allowed, you should notify your supervisor as soon as possible. As reassembly after a repair is usually the final operation before valeting, it may be very close to the time when the customer has been told to collect their car. A customer arriving at your workshop to pick up their vehicle will not be too pleased if they have not been told in advance that it is not ready. An early indication to your supervisor will allow him time to contact the customer to arrange a later time for collection, thus preventing an angry customer having to go away and return later or on another day.

Remember, an angry customer is not a satisfied customer and word of mouth usually travels fast around his friends, who may also be your potential customers.

*A2.2.10   Replacement activities are performed in accordance with
statutory and organisational policy and procedure for health
and safety*

Refer to *A2.1.9*

REPAIR BODY PANELS

A3.1   PREPARE VEHICLE FOR REPAIR OF BODY PANELS

A3.1.1   Appropriate information is accessed from appropriate sources to inform the required preparation activities

The repair of body panels differs from that of replacement in that no two types of damage will be the same, so no exact repair operation will be available to instruct in the repair procedure. Nevertheless, general guide lines on repair procedures will be available in body repair text books or from product or tool manufacturers.

To establish what type of repair will be required to be carried out on a body panel, refer to details on the job card and the estimate for the vehicle being repaired.

A3.1.2   Protective clothing and equipment appropriate to the preparation activities are used

The method used in the preparation of body panels will depend upon the type of repair being carried out. Therefore the type of protective clothing and equipment may differ from one repair situation to another.

Examples of the preparation methods are:
- Chemical paint stripping.
- Mechanical grinding and sanding.
- Shot/grit blasting
- Abrasive papers and cloths

The preparation methods can be divided into two main types:
- Chemical preparation
- Abrasive preparation

Taking each in turn:

Chemical Preparation

Paint and surface coatings can be removed using a chemical paint remover, during which procedure the operator should use the following safety and protective clothing and equipment:

Rubber gloves and apron - these must be made from a rubber material that will withstand attack from the chemicals used. They will prevent the paint stripper being absorbed into your overalls or clothes, which, if you come into contact with a sound-painted surface at a later stage, may cause unnecessary damage to that surface. Rubber gloves will prevent contact with your skin.

Breathing and filter masks are not required, but the paint stripper should be used in a well-ventilated area. Clear goggles must be worn to prevent splashes into your eyes.

When using metal pre-treatment solution based on phosphoric acid during the preparation of bare LCS surfaces, the same safety precaution and equipment should be used as that for paint strippers.

Mechanical/Abrasion Preparation

During the preparation of panel surfaces using many of the abrasives available there are added dangers of dirt, dust, grit and metal particles being air borne. For this reason, alternative types of safety equipment and clothing should be used.

When using sanders and grinders, it is a requirement under the COSHH regulations to use equipment that is connected to a *dust- extraction system*.

When abrading, good-quality clear *safety goggles* must be worn.

Cotton overalls, leather gloves and *safety footwear* will protect against metal that has become hot by friction, against any sharp edges or against your clothes or skin being burnt from sparks during grinding. A suitable *particle mask* must also be worn, especially when shot/grit blasting.

When grinding, remove or cover up any flammable materials that may be damaged by the grinding sparks, cover up all windows with a suitable cover, as the sparks will burn into the glass and their marks will become very difficult to remove.

Do not grind or abrade in close proximity to any flammable liquids, such as petrol or paint thinner, as this poses a high fire risk. If at all possible, a fume extractor or portable ventilator should be used.

A3.1.3   *Surfaces and structures are clean and free from materials likely to hinder repair*

Before the preparation of a body panel surface, any material that may hinder this repair must be removed. Any dirt or mud on the panel must be removed. It may also be necessary to remove under-body sealant, sound-deadening pads, coach lines, rubber scuff strips, badges and lamps if they are likely to be a hindrance during the repair process.

A3.1.4 Surface finishes are removed, where required, using approved methods and equipment

Body panels are repaired for one of two reasons. They have sustained damage as a result of an accident or they have corroded.

The method used to remove the surface finish will depend upon the type and size of damage being repaired. The paint should be removed from some distance around the repair and from the undamaged part of the panel. This is to allow all repair work to be carried out on unpainted metal surfaces.

Normally, chemical paint stripping is chosen when the complete panel has to be stripped without causing any scratch damage to the sound metal surface. This method may be chosen when there is evidence of paint faults such as flaking, or light surface oxide under the paint finish.

A guide to follow for chemical paint stripping may be:

a. Select and use all the safety equipment and clothing listed in *A3.1.2.*

b. Protect all areas around the damaged panel with masking materials to prevent any accidental splashing from the paint stripper.

c. Some paint finishes may require to be scuffed with coarse abrasive to break the surface skin.

d. Using a long-handled brush, apply the paint stripper to the affected area, allowing a few minutes for the paint stripper to take effect.

e. Using a flat metal paint scraper, scrape off the paint on to a suitable paper or cardboard sheet laid on the floor. This will prevent any contaminated paint stripper being stood on and carried on the soles of your boots.It may be necessary to repeat (d) and (e) depending on the type and thickness of the paint being removed.

f. Once all the paint has been removed thoroughly, wash the panel with water to remove all traces of residue from the surface. Failure to complete this stage thoroughly may result in future paint coats flaking or not fully hardening when applied to the panel surface.

g. Remove the masking and check that all traces of the paint remover have been thoroughly cleared away. The surface should now be ready for the next stage in the repair/repaint process.

Mechanical/Abrasive Methods

When removing surface finishes using abrasives, whether by hand or by power tools, all the safety procedures stated in *3.1.2* should be followed.

The type and extent of damage will be the major factors in determining the equipment used in the surface finish removal.

Using abrasives for this operation can be divided into two main systems:

    a. By hand tools - using abrasive papers and files

    b. By power tools - grinding, sanding and grit/shot blasting.

Hand Tools

This method may be used only when small areas require to be prepared or for the removal of material in areas inaccessible using power tools. The abrasive material used during this operation will be restricted to P40 or P80 grit aluminium-oxide production paper.

Power Tools

Grinding - This is the most severe method of material removal usually confined to the removal of surplus metal, welds or even metal cutting. It is not a recommended method of surface finish removal as it may dig into the thin metal panel surface, thus requiring extra unnecessary filling during the preparation stage.

Sanding - The most popular method used when sanding to remove surface finishes is with a fibre disc fitted to a disc sander. These fibre discs are supplied in grits ranging from 24 to 100. One point to bear in mind is that the coarser the disc used, the larger the scratches you will have to fill during the preparation stage. This is more so if you are removing paint from aluminium or plastic surfaces.

Using a dual-action sander fitted with production paper or open coat abrasive discs will give a smoother finish and require less preparation during the refinishing stages. This method may take longer than using a disc sander.

Shot/grit blasting - Removing surface finishes by this method will leave the most uniform finish with the least refinish preparation required. Shot/grit blasting is ideal for the removal of pitted rust on a metal surface, due to the ability of the small grit particles to blast into the smallest area. To avoid unnecessary mess, it is advisable to use a shot/grit blaster that will catch and re-cycle the grit.

When removing surface finishes, either for accident damage repair or for rust repair, an area of undamaged surface around the repair area should be cleared so that you are working on bare metal or plastic surfaces only.

A3.1.5 *Surfaces and structures not subject to repair are protected*

When carrying out paint surface finish removal it is important that you protect all areas not requiring repair from any damage that may occur during the removal operation.

Chemical Paint Strippers

All areas adjacent to or surrounding the repair area should be masked off with suitable water-resistant paper or polythene sheets. This will prevent any splashing or over-applying of the paint stripper.

Any crevices, door, boot or bonnet checks should be blocked off to prevent any of the paint stripper being trapped as this may be difficult to remove or even missed during the cleaning-up process.

Grinding

The greatest problem associated with grinding is of sparks from the grinder striking paintwork or glass where they will burn into the paint or glass which will cause damage very difficult to remove. A suitable anti-spark cover should be placed over areas that are vulnerable to being struck by sparks.

Sanding

Typical areas that may be unnecessarily damaged by sanding scratch marks would be mouldings, window rubbers, bumpers and the edges of adjacent panels. To protect against accidental scratch damage, one or two layers of masking tape should be applied around the edges of the components. Alternatively remove the items if possible.

Shot/Grit Blasting

The protection described for grinding and sanding should be used when shot/grit blasting, with the addition that any areas of the engine where sand or grit particles may be drawn in should be blocked off, this will include areas such as carburettor or air intake, oil filler and dip-stick hole. Any grit that does get drawn into the engine can cause excessive internal damage.

A3.1.6   Preparation of surfaces is completed within approved
timescales
Refer to *A2.1.7.*

A3.1.7   Where preparation of surfaces is likely to exceed the approved
timescale, the circumstances are reported promptly to an
authorised person
Refer to *A2.1.8.*

A3.1.8   Preparation is performed in accordance with statutory and
organisational policy and procedure for health and safety
Refer to *A2.1.9*

A3:2 REINSTATE CONDITION OF BODY PANELS

A3.2.1 *Appropriate information is accessed from appropriate sources*
to inform the required repair activity
Refer to *A3.1.1*.

A3.2.2 *Protective clothing and equipment appropriate to the repair*
activities are used
Refer to *A3.1.2*.

A3.2.3 *Repair equipment is prepared in accordance with*
manufacturers' specification
The choice of repair equipment will depend upon the following:
a. The type of repair - that is, accident damage or corrosion repairs.
b. The extent of the repair - that is, minor or major repairs.
c. The availability of repair sections.

The equipment selected for each repair will vary from hand tools to electrical and pneumatic power tools, to MAGS welding, oxy-acetylene welding and plasma-cutting equipment. It is important that, whatever type of equipment you choose, it is prepared for use in accordance with the manufacturers' specifications. Failure to do so may result in damage to the equipment, damage to the tools or injury to the operator.

Minor Damage Repair
Minor damage may be repaired using a selection of hammers and dollies; the choice of hammer and dolly combination being dependent on the shape and contour of the panel being repaired. For areas of body panels that are inaccessible to reach using a dolly, it may be easier to use one of the many body-pry spoons available. A range of body spoons, hammers and dollies is shown later in this section.

The machined faces of hammers, dollies and body spoons should always be kept free from marks, chips and debris. Hammer shafts should be free from cracks and if they break should be replaced using the one specified for the hammer. This is important as the shaft used will depend upon the size and weight of the hammer head.

To facilitate beating out the damaged area where access is limited at the rear of a body panel, hydraulic spreader jaws may be used, provided there is a suitably strong support at the rear of the damaged area. Any high-pressure hydraulic reforming equipment should be free from oil leaks and

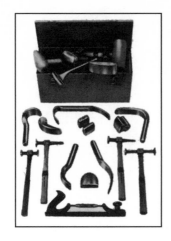

Sykes-Pickavant body repair tool sets

the hydraulic pipe should be free from any damage. This type of
equipment should be serviced on a regular basis. Hydraulic push rams
have a selection of extension tubes and various shaped heads that are held

together using a screw or snap fit. When assembling a certain combination ensure they are securely fitted together.

Hot-air guns may be used to reform minor damage to plastic bumpers. When preparing electric hot-air guns, ensure cables and plugs are securely fitted and free from damage.

Have a selection of nozzles at hand, which will aid in the direction and concentration of the hot-air jet. If the hot-air gun has an adjustable heat control, select the correct heat control and adjust before using.

During the repair of minor damage using hammers and dollies, stretching of the damaged area may occur. This may be reduced using the hot-shrinking technique. To carry this out you will need a boxwood mallet, hammer and dolly, oxy-acetylene blow torch, cold water and a sponge. Have all this equipment and tools at hand, as this process is very quick and if time is lost the shrinking process may not be as effective as required. It may be advisable to wear a leather glove on the hand holding the dolly to prevent you being burnt by the hot metal during the shrinking process. Before using oxy-acetylene heating equipment, check for gas leaks, ensure tubes are free from cuts or fractures and ensure the gas bottles are securely fitted into their trolley.

Corrosion Repairs

When corrosion is found on a body panel the most successful method of repair would be to replace the complete panel. Alternatively repair sections may be available or you may have to fabricate your own repair section. For a temporary short-term repair, polyester body fillers and fibre bridging fillers may be used.

The tools required when carrying out part-panel replacement or patching of a corroded body panel will include: hammers, rulers, scribes, drills, tin snips, hacksaw, hand or pneumatic grinder, oxy-acetylene and MAGS welding equipment, mole/vice grip and clamps. As with all other tools, they should only be used for the purpose for which they were intended and used in a safe and efficient manner. This is even more important when using compressed gases stored in cylinders such as oxygen , acetylene and angon or CO_2. These gases are completely safe provided they are not abused - remember that they are stored in cylinders pressurised between 250 psi and 2500 psi.

Repair To Plastic Components

The general damage to plastic components will usually result in the components being replaced. Nevertheless, minor damage to bumpers, such as splits and small dents, can be successfully repaired using hot air and hot-air plastic welding equipment. Before using this equipment you will have to determine the type of plastic being repaired, as each plastic reacts differently under varying temperature ranges. The correct heat setting is therefore very important.

See the list of plastic types in *A3.2.4*.

3.2.4 Components are reinstated using approved methods and equipment

When repairing vehicle body panels, it would be advisable where possible to carry out these repairs with the panels in situ. Unfortunately, it may not always be possible to gain access to the rear of panels to facilitate repairs. In this case, any bolt-on panels may be removed. For procedures in the removal and replacement of bolt-on panels refer to *A2.1.3* and *A2.2.5*.

Minor Damage Repair

Minor damage is a result of sheet metal being deformed beyond its elastic limit. When a panel is damaged in this way, the area around the damage will become stiff and lose its elasticity. These stiff creased areas will have become work-hardened due to a change in the grain structure of the sheet metal.

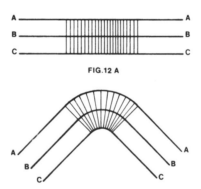

Change in the grain structure of the sheet metal

In order to rectify this type of damage, repairs should be carried out using a reverse force to that which caused the damage, so a true assessment of the damage must be made. Rectification of panel damage can be divided into two stages:

i. *Roughing out or straightening the damaged sections and panels to their approximate shape.* This is done using a heavy blunt-shaped dolly or a specially-designed roughing out hammer. Do not be tempted at this stage to use the ball end of a heavy ball pein hammer as this may lead to excessive stretching of the damaged area which will require more unnecessary work during the finishing stage. The roughing out process should be carried out using the minimum number of blows possible.

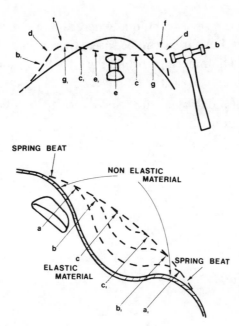

Straightening the damaged sections and panels to their approximate shape

ii. *Finishing and preparing the surface to a smooth finish using a selection of finishing hammers and dollies.* The choice of hammer and dolly will depend on the shape of the panel surface. As a rough guide to hammer selection, choose one which has a flat face for slightly crowned surfaces, and a slightly crowned hammer for flat surfaces. This will help prevent hammer marks during the dressing (planishing) process.

The technique of hammer-finishing a panel surface can be divided into two:

- Direct hammering
- Indirect hammering

Whichever technique is used, again care should be taken not to cause any unnecessary stretching of the metal surface.

Direct hammering is a technique which involves the dolly being held directly under the damaged area and the hammer being used in direct contact with the dolly, with the metal panel's surface in between. As the hammer and dolly are moved around the damaged area, you should hear a slight dinging noise as the hammer and dolly come into contact.

Indirect hammering is a technique where the hammering takes place just off the dolly. Low areas can be raised by pushing up with the dolly block and lightly hammering around the edge thus producing a reverse force to that which caused the damage.

Final dressing of a damaged surface will normally involve a combination of direct and indirect hammering.

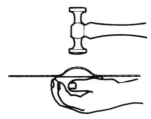

Direct hammering

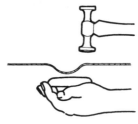

Indirect hammering

On panel surfaces where large shallow dents occur, a long ridge (high area) may appear around the damaged area. This can be reduced using light hammer blows in conjunction with a spring hammer blade, which has the effect of spreading the force of the blows on the surface.

After planishing is complete, any high or low spots can be highlighted using a flexible body file. Unfortunately, the gauge of metal used to manufacture modern motor vehicle body panels does not allow final finishing using a body file. Once you are satisfied that the surface is as

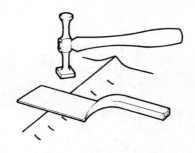

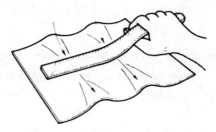

Spring hammering

close to its original contour as possible, it can be final-finished using a proprietary-brand polyester body filler or stopper. Should the metal become stretched during the planishing stages of the repair, it will have to be shrunk, using either the hot or cold shrinking technique. A brief description is detailed below.

The tools used for hot shrinking will be oxy-acetylene heating torch, mallet, planishing shrinking hammer, selection of dollies, wire brush scraper, water and a damp cloth. The wire brush and scraper are used to remove any unwanted sound deadening or sealer from the underside of the panel. Before starting the hot-shrinking process, lay out all your tools and equipment close to hand. This will allow you to go from one tool to another quickly as speed is very impotant to ensure success with this process. Once you have located the centre of the stretched area, heat a small spot about the size of a 10p piece (10mm to 15mm) to a cherry red colour, holding the dolly loosely under this hot spot. Using the mallet, place a few heavy blows quickly around the perimeter of the hot spot. This will force the stretched surplus metal into the hot spot. This must all happen while the metal is still red hot.

When the surplus metal is gathered in the centre of the hot spot the final blow should be in the centre. When the hot spot has turned black it should be quenched using a sponge or cloth soaked in cold water. After it has

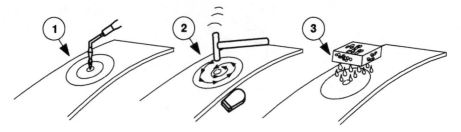

1. Spot heating (to bright red). 2. Apply hammer blows, proceeding in a coil shape round the heated spot, using a wooden or aluminium hammer and a dolly. 3. Cooling.

cooled final planishing can take place, as previously described. If further stretched metal exists, repeat this operation until it has returned to its original condition. Stretched metal can also be reduced using the cold-striking technique. This differs from hot shrinking in that the stretched metal is hammered into a groove in the shrinking dolly and final finishing is by filling the groove with body solder or polyester filler.

Hydraulic Reforming

Many areas of minor damage may require the use of hydraulic reforming equipment. This equipment can be used to push or pull a body panel into position, with the use of hydraulic rams operated by a hand pump, various extension tubes and shaped ends that are either screwed on or are a snap-fit. For areas that have limited space, the use of spreader jaws will assist in correcting accidental damage - an example of this may be within a door shell or between a double-skinned panel.

One basic principle to remember when using this type of equipment is that the corrective forces should be applied as close as possible to the centre of the damage and in a direction opposite to that of the impact.

When body jacking your must ensure that the anchor point that you choose is strong enough to support the push without causing any further damage.

The use of a rubber head fitted to the body jack or a selection of wooden blocks will help prevent damage. Typical areas suitable for use as an anchor point may be an inner wheel arch, chassis leg or chassis cross-member. From these points, it should be possible to reform the shape of a front or rear wing, front and rear lower valance, bonnet slam panel, head lamp support panel or a rear boot slam panel. When carrying out a push-or-pull, it is wise to carry it out in stages. If you push too far it will be very difficult to bring the area back to its required position.

To prevent this happening, apply the force and push the damaged area until it looks close to its original position. Release the pressure and watch how much the damaged area returns. This is due to the elasticity of the metal. With the pressure taken off, check all the alignments; it may be necessary to re-apply more pressure and push a bit further. Carry out this operation as many times as required until the damaged area is re-aligned.

Portable hydraulic repair equipment and accessories

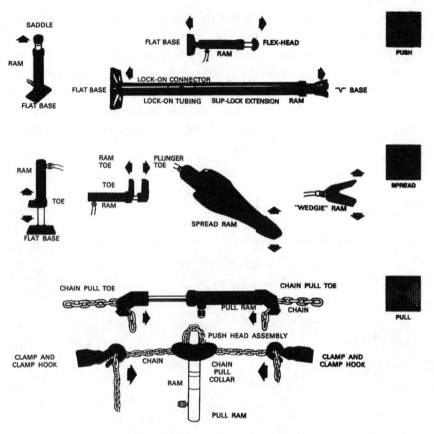

Basic set-ups using Porto-Power rams and attachments

Plastic Reforming

Plastics fall into two main categories:

i. Thermo setting plastics

These plastics are usually very hard and, when damaged during accident collision, they will snap or shatter. Thermo setting plastics cannot be repaired using welding or thermal reforming. Any repair required will be carried out using epoxy-resin based adhesives. Any major damage to this category of plastic will usually render it uneconomical to repair and it will require a replacement part.

ii. Thermo Plastic Plastics

Thermo plastics can usually be repaired or reformed using the hot-air technique. One of the major problems associated with thermo plastics is in the identification of the plastic type. This is important because there are approximately eight different plastics within this group and each one may require a different temperature or alteration to the welding technique used.

One other important factor to remember when carrying out a plastic weld is that you must use a filler rod that is of the same composition as the parent plastic.

A list of the plastic types and a typical application for each is shown later.

When determining whether or not it is viable to repair a plastic component, you should take into consideration the length of time required to prepare and carry out the actual repair, as well as the fact that all visible parts of the plastic component will have to be refinished by either repainting or re-texturing to match their original appearance.

Many people within the body-repair industry are reluctant to repair plastic components and will always argue for a replacement part. Typical examples of where a plastic repair would be justified could be:

- A small crack on a bumper or grille
- A locating lug broken off a plastic headlamp casing
- A cracked or broken heater box.

It is important that you understand the reasons behind the need for automotive plastic repair and the pressures that have brought about its development:

- The increasing cost of new plastic components.
- The serious problems posed with disposal of plastic waste.
- The environmental pressures being applied to the insurance industry.
- The increasing quantity of plastic components used per vehicle.

On the following pages Protoplas has set out information regarding the various categories of plastics.

One thing to bear in mind is that plastic welding and reforming is not beyond the abilities of any person who is familiar with and employed within a practical discipline. Normally a short two-day course will equip you with enough knowledge to be able to carry out many minor repairs and with continual practice you will become very proficient in a short time.

It should be noted that the repair of plastics is not limited solely to the automotive industry and any techniques and methods learned can be adapted to many other industries; such as, farming, factory maintenance engineers, plumbers and water board technicians, cleansing departments

continues on page 51

IDENTIFICATION PROCEDURES

Plastics react in a hot air stream in the following ways:-

(ABS) Acrylonitrile Butadiene Styrene

    Bubbles - distinctive smell.

(PA) Polyamide

    Bubbles and spits - high temperature. Turns grey or brown.

(PC) Polycarbonate/Xenoy

    Bubbles.

(PE) Polyethylene

    When heated becomes clear.

(PP) Polypropylene/EPDM

    Forms web rings in wash, sticky. Becomes wet.

(PVC) Polyvinyl Chloride

    Burns brown - strong pungent small.

(TPUR) Polyurethane

    Smokes and smoulders. Surface degrades.

APPLICATIONS & GUN SET CHART FOR PLASTICS IN AUTOMOTIVE USE

CODE	MATERIAL NAME	CHEMICAL CAUTION	APPLICATIONS	WELD TEMP	WELD SET	TACK SET	SPEED - 3MM SET	SPEED - 5MM SET
ABS	Acronitrile Butadiene Styrene	Resistance to petrol & alcohol for short period only.	Grilles. Vent panels. Side/tail lamp backs. Trim moulding.	350°C	4.5	4.5	4.5	5
PA	Polyamide	Good resistance.	Used in areas of high temps. & impact vulnerable areas, e.g. Radiator tank, Wheel trims.	400°C	5.5	5.5	5.5	6
PC PO or PBTP	Polycarbonate Pocan Xenoy PC Alloy	Vulnerable to petrol & brake fluid.	Major bumper units usually painted. Door handles. Front & rear mouldings.	400°C	5	5	5.5	5.5
PE	Polyethylene high and low density.	Good resistance	Air intakes. Stone guards. Fluid bottles.	350°C	4.5	4.5	5	5.5
PMMA	Polymethyl-methacrylate (Acrylic)	Resistance to solvents for short period only. Use only white spirit to clean.	Side/tail lenses	350°C	4	4	4.5	5

47

IDENTIFICATION, APPLICATIONS & GUN SET CHART FOR PLASTICS IN AUTOMOTIVE USE - Contd.

CODE	MATERIAL NAME	CHEMICAL CAUTION	APPLICATIONS	WELD TEMP	WELD SET.	TACK SET	SPEED - 3MM SET	SPEED - 5MM SET
PP	Polypropylene	Good resistance to solvents & chemicals. Resistant to acid.	Wide range of uses, e.g. Bumpers, Housings, Scuff panels. Trim panels. Splash shields. Rubbing strips. Stone guards. Fan cowls, Grilles Fluid bottles. Sill covers. Arch flares.	350°	5	5	5.5	5.5
EPDM	Modified Ethylene Diene Rubber	Good resistance	Bumpers	350°C	5	5	5.5	5.5
PVC	Polyvinyl Chloride	Poor solvent resistance. Good chemical resistance.	Soft upholstery covering. Some dashboard parts.	300°C	4	4	4.5	4.5
TPUR	Theroplastic Polyurethane	Resistant to petrol & alcohol for short period only.	Front panel/bumper units. Large flexible bumpers. Soft bezels. Rubbing strips. Styling aprons/skirts.	Due to the nature of TPUR it is very difficult to weld. A more successful repair is effected by using a flexible bonding method.				

48

IDENTIFICATION, APPLICATIONS & GUN SET CHART FOR PLASTICS IN AUTOMOTIVE USE - Contd.

CODE	MATERIAL NAME	CHEMICAL CAUTION	APPLICATIONS	WELD TEMP	WELD SET	TACK SET	SPEED - 3 MM SET	SPEED - 5MM SET
PUR Foam	Polyurethane Expanded Foam	Resistant to petrol & alcohol for short period.	Boot spoilers. Internal bumper cores.	Repair by flexible bonding.				
SMC	Sheet Moulded Compound	Good resistance to chemicals & solvents.	Bumpers. Bonnets. Tail Gates. Cab bodies. Sump guards. Cooling fan support.	Repair as Glass Reinforced Polyester.				
TSP	Thermo-set Plastic	Good resistance to chemicals & solvents.	Electrical switchgear housings. Handles/levers.	Repair with hard setting epoxy.				
GRP	Glass reinforced Polyester.	Good resistance to solvents.	Small production vehicle bodies. Styling aprons/skirts.	Repair using GRP repair method.				

COMMON AUTOMOTIVE USES OF PLASTICS

Automotive, Commercial, Motorcycle and Farming

Car

BUMPERS:	EPDM PC PUR PP SMC
BODY PANELS:	PC PP SMC PUR
GRILLES:	ABS PP PA
FAN COWLINGS:	PP PA
H'LAMP BUCKETS:	PP SM
SIDE LAMPS	ABS PP
INDICATORS:	ABS P
RADIATOR TANKS:	PA
EXPANSION TANK:	PP
FLUID BOTTLES:	PP PEHD
AIR FILTER HOUSINGS:	PP
HOUSINGS:	PP PEHD
SPLASH GUARDS:	PP PEHD
BATTERY:	PP
SCUTTLE PANELS:	ABS PP PA
HEATER BOX:	PP
DASH:	SOFT-PVC PP
DASH INSERTS:	ABS PP
INTERNAL TRIM:	PP ABS SOFT-PVC
TAIL LIGHTS:	ABS
BODY TRIMMING:	ABS PP SOFT-PVC PC SMC
WHEEL COVERS:	ABS PA PC PP
FUEL TANKS:	PEHD
BODY STYLING:	PUR GRP ABS PP PA
BOOT SPOILERS:	PUR-FOAM PUR GRP ABS
WING MIRRORS:	PA ABS PP

Motor Cycle

FAIRINGS:	ABS SMC GRP P
COVER PANELS:	ABS PP PEHD
SEAT COWLS:	ABS GRP PP
SEAT PAN	PP PEHD SMC
FUEL TANKS	PEHD
MUD GUARDS:	ABS PP PEHD
BELLY PANS:	ABS PP PEHD
HEAD LAMP SHELLS:	ABS PP
TAIL LAMPS:	PP ABS
INDICATORS:	ABS PP
GRILLES:	PP ABS
FLUID BOTTLES:	PP PEHD
BATTERY:	PP
CASINGS:	PP PEHD ABS
WING MIRRORS	ABS PP PA PC

Commercial Vehicles

BUMPERS:	SMC GRP RUBBER
BODY PANELS:	SMC
GRILLES:	ABS PP PA SMC
MUD GUARDS	PEHD PP RUBBER
CAB BODIES	SMC

Apart from the above additions most commercial
plastic parts are made of the same range of
plastics as used in cars.

* * * * * * *

(wheely bins) and any other area where plastic is a widely-used material. This is because many of the thermo-plastics used in the automotive industry are the same as those used in these other industries.

Corrosion Damage Repair

When a motor vehicle panel is damaged by corrosion the only permanent cure would be to replace the panel. However, it is not always economically viable to justify panel replacement. Other repair techniques which would act as a temporary repair would be:

- Patching, using glass reinforced plastic (GRP) lay-up system finished off with a polyester filler. This type of repair will probably last the longest of any polyester repair technique. This is because the set GRP is non-porous and will hold back moisture longer.
- Chopped GRP bridging filler finished off with a polyester fill. This technique will offer similar resistance to the corrosion but is still only regarded as a temporary repair method.
- Polyester body filler only. This is the least successful method of corrosion repair as the filler is porous and will absorb moisture, thus allowing the corrosion to restart quickly.
- Patching by cutting out the corroded area, fabricating a repair section with material the same as the parent metal and completely welding into position. Sanding and finishing with polyester filler or body solder prior to refinishing. With this method it is important to completely seal the underside of the repair with a suitable sealant, as the protection will have been burnt off during the welding process. Where the metal is damaged by surface corrosion and this damage has only caused light pitting and the metal is not perforated, all traces of the corrosion should be removed by either mechanical sanding or by the use of portable shot/grit blaster, the latter being more effective as it leaves the surface with a uniform finish free from sanding scratch marks which will require filling. The grit is also more efficient at removing corrosion from the pits in the metal surface. Before any priming and repainting of the bare surface takes place, it is wise to treat with a phosphoric acid based metal pre-treatment solution which will help prevent further corrosion reforming.

A3.2.5   Where repair of components includes disturbance to electrical, mechanical or electronic systems, appropriate authorised assistance is sought where required

During the repair of body panels, it may be necessary to disconnect, remove or partly dismantle some of the mechanical, electrical or electronic systems that are located within, or close to, the repair area. This may be to prevent damage from hammer blows, burning when welding or causing an obstruction when using hydraulic reforming equipment. The nature of the disturbance to these systems can be as minor as pulling a wiring loom to one side and as major as the complete removal of a full electronic system. Some of this extra disturbance you may find quite simple and well within your capacity, whereas the complete removal of an electronic system may be outside your capabilities. If this is the case, and if you feel in any doubt, you should seek assistance from someone who is a specialist in this area. It is better to allow someone else who has the necessary knowledge and experience to do this part of the work for you, rather than to try to do it yourself, with the possibility of causing extensive damage to the component or unit you want removed. Any unnecessary damage caused by you will have to be made good by your company, which will then find itself running at a loss or a very low profit margin.

A3.2.6   *The repair of components is completed within the approved timescales*
Refer to *A2.1.7*.

A3.2.7   *Where repair of components is likely to exceed the approved timescale, the circumstances are reported promptly to an authorised person*
Refer to *A2.1.8*.

A3.2.8   *The completed repair is passed to the next stage of the process to schedule and in a condition which enables the process to continue*
When a vehicle is in the workshop for repair, it is very unlikely that the full job will be done from start to finish by the one technician. Being a body repairer you will only be concerned with all repair work, including filling, but not priming or painting, which will be carried out by a vehicle refinisher/painter. It is important that you complete your part of the repair within the allocated time scale and to a suitable standard to allow the vehicle to proceed to the next stage on time. This is extremely important to the workshop controller, who will try to ensure that the repair shop and paint shop work to their full capacity. This can only be achieved where the flow of work from one workshop to another is uninterrupted and all repair jobs are completed on time. Failure to do so

will result in the refinish shop having quiet spells and then be overloaded, which has the effect of vehicles not being ready when promised to the customer.

A3.2.9   *Repair activities are performed in accordance with statutory and organisational policy and procedures for health and safety*
     Refer to *A2.1.9*

A4L UNDERPINNING KNOWLEDGE

RECTIFY BODY MISALIGNMENT AND REPAIR/REPLACE BODY SECTIONS

A4.1 REINSTATE UNDERBODY AND BODYSHELL ALIGNMENT

A4.1.1   Appropriate information is accessed from appropriate sources to inform the procedures for the reinstatement of alignment

When carrying out re-alignment to a unitary body, it will be necessary to compare the dimensions of the damage with the original measurements, which will have been researched and printed on data sheets produced by companies such as Autodata, Thatchams and the vehicle manufacturer.

If your company has a body-alignment jig, details of dimensions and alignment are also available from this. The alignment jig manufacturers will also provide information on procedures for the reinstatement of any misalignment found.

A4.1.2   Protective clothing and equipment appropriate to the repair activities are used

Refer to Unit *A13* and *A2.1.2* for general awareness. When carrying out underbody and bodyshell alignment, it may be necessary for you to raise the vehicle to inspect, measure and work under it. This may be carried out by one of the following methods:

Hydraulic Jack

When using a hydraulic jack, you must first ensure it is designed to lift the weight of the vehicle you are working on. To do this you must check the safe working load (SWL) of the jack, which should be marked on the jack. Check to ensure there are no oil leaks from the jack and, if there are, do not use it. When raising the vehicle, jack from a suitable support on the vehicle chassis or axle. Never jack from an engine or transmission component. When the vehicle is raised from the ground it should be supported on axle stands. Again check the SWL of the stands to ensure they will cope with the weight of the vehicle.

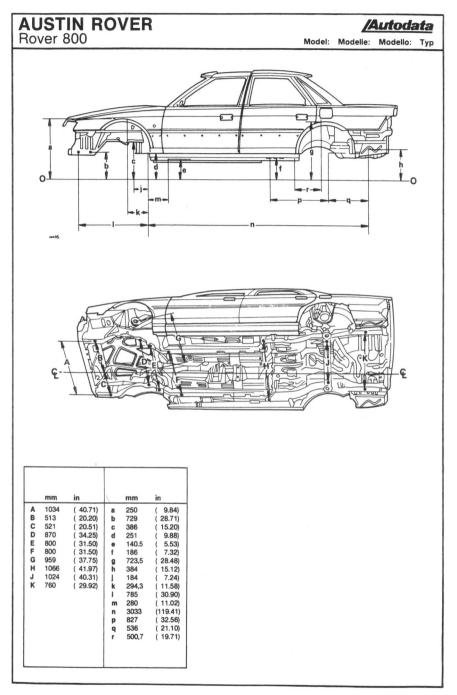

AUSTIN ROVER
Rover 800

Autodata

	mm	in		mm	in
A	1034	(40.71)	**a**	250	(9.84)
B	513	(20.20)	**b**	729	(28.71)
C	521	(20.51)	**c**	386	(15.20)
D	870	(34.25)	**d**	251	(9.88)
E	800	(31.50)	**e**	140.5	(5.53)
F	800	(31.50)	**f**	186	(7.32)
G	959	(37.75)	**g**	723,5	(28.48)
H	1066	(41.97)	**h**	384	(15.12)
J	1024	(40.31)	**j**	184	(7.24)
K	760	(29.92)	**k**	294,3	(11.58)
			l	785	(30.90)
			m	280	(11.02)
			n	3033	(119.41)
			p	827	(32.56)
			q	536	(21.10)
			r	500,7	(19.71)

Details of dimensions for Austin Rover 800, prepared by Autodata

Important Note: *Never go under, or work under, a vehicle that has been raised using a hydraulic jack without supporting the vehicle on stands.*

Vehicle Lift (Ramp)

As with the hydraulic jack, the ramp must be able to raise the vehicle you are working on. The SWL will also be marked on the ramp. When the vehicle is on the ramp, put on the hand brake, or if the brakes are inoperative chalk the wheels to prevent the vehicle from moving. When the ramp is raised, there should be stops both front and back to prevent the vehicle rolling off the ramp should you require to move it slightly while it is raised.

A4.1.3   Equipment selected for the assessment of vehicle alignment is appropriate to the vehicle manufacturers' specification

The type and selection of the equipment used to check misalignment will largely depend on the extent of the damage. Alignment measuring equipment can be as simple as a home-made set of trammels, gun sight gauges or drop-check (using a plumb bob and chalk line), or as complex as sophisticated computerised alignment and recording equipment such as the 'Car-O-Tronic' by Car-O-Liner.

When assessing body misalignment using trammels, gun sight gauges or the drop-check measurement system, you will be relying on your own judgement and your line of sight. Some measurements may be taken from the manufacturer's or Autodata publication.

When assessing body misalignment using one of the many body jigs available, you will be comparing the extent of damage against sizes illustrated on the data sheet for the specific make and model provided by the jig manufacturer. The information that is provided on the data sheet is a result of extensive research by the jig manufacturer and the vehicle manufacturer. By adhering to the measurements stated on the data sheet you will be measuring in accordance with the vehicle manufacturer's specifications.

A4.1.4   Equipment used for the assessment of vehicle alignment is prepared and adjusted in accordance with the equipment manufacturers' specification

Whichever equipment you use to assess body misalignment, you must stick strictly to the instructions laid down by the manufacturer. Failure to

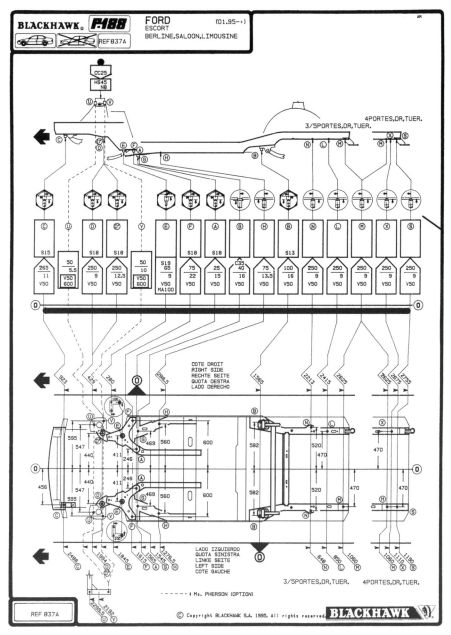

Measurement data used in the Blackhawk measurement system

do so may result in incorrect measurements, which could result in the vehicle being incorrectly re-aligned. The equipment instruction book will give step-by-step procedures for the preparation and adjustment of its use.

You may find that you have had experience using one type of equipment but are unfamiliar with new equipment bought, or you have changed employment to an employer who has a different type of measuring equipment. Do not be put of by this as the principle for measuring is very similar between manufacturers. If your company has purchased a new type of measuring/alignment jig training is usually provided by the manufacturer but complete confidence is gained by continual use. During the period which you gain experience and confidence you will find yourself referring to the instruction manual many times, but this will become less through time. It is better to refer to these publications and make a good quality repair than to use guess work and struggle with the equipment.

A4.1.5 *The vehicle is prepared and, where appropriate, installed/located on the alignment equipment in accordance with the equipment manufacturers' instructions*

Before mounting a vehicle on to an alignment jig you will have to select the appropriate data sheet for the vehicle you are going to repair. The information you will require to allow you to mount the vehicle will be:

- Special mounting brackets.
- Locations and spacing for all clamps.
- Procedure for raising the vehicle and mounting on the jig.

Depending on the type and manufacturer of the equipment in use, there may be various methods of mounting the vehicle on the jig. The Car-O-Liner system lists five methods of setting up the vehicle. They are:

a. Using a jack only.
b. Using a jack and wheel stands.
c. Using a two-column lift or fork lift.
d. Using the integral Car-O-Liner scissor lift TS and run-up kit T49.
e. Using the integral Car-O-Liner scissor lift TS and run-up kit TSS.

An example of the mounting procedure using the jack and wheel stands is:

a. Jack up the vehicle and place on wheel stands or ordinary axle stands.
b. Roll the bench (with wheels on ends) into position under the vehicle. Try to place the centre line of the vehicle and bench as close together as possible. Position the car, in the longitudinal direction to facilitate work on the damaged area with the draw aligner.

2 USING JACK AND WHEEL STAND

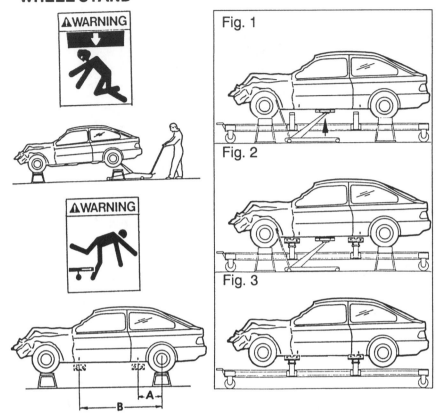

Setting up the vehicle on the bench using jack and wheel stand

c. Mark the sill clamp dimensions A and B (see data sheet) with chalk or tape. The vehicle must be on its suspension. Clean away underbody compound and dirt to give the sill clamp a good grip and to give the correct vertical dimensions.

d. Slide the bench mountings along the tracks to the positions marked 'A' and 'B' for the sill clamps. If the distance between the bench mounting and the vehicle is too little, use a jack (see Figs 1 - 3).

e. Lift the bench towards the vehicle, making sure that the sill flanges fit properly into the sill clamps, then lift the car high enough to allow the wheel stand to be removed.

f. Remove the wheel stands and lower the bench to the floor.

g. Tighten the bench mounting and sill clamps in the correct sequence (see diagram fig 4).

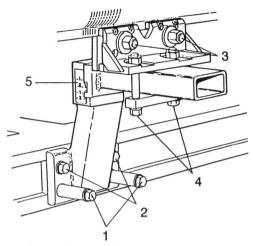

Correct sequence for tightening bench mounting and sill clamps

The above description is only one method of mounting one manufacturer's jig. There are variations between jig types and between manufacturers.

A4.1.6 *The nature and extent of misalignment is determined using approved methods*

When selecting and using equipment to determine the extent of misalignment, the severity of the damage will determine the equipment that you will use. A visual inspection may show that there is no apparent structural damage, so you may be able to carry out your assessment using fairly basic tools, such as a tape rule, trammels or gun sight gauges. Typical visual checks could be:

- Space between rear of wheel and wheel arch - this could be compared from side to side.
- Check distance between centres of wheels on each side (a simple piece of string could do this)
- The gaps around doors, boot lids and bonnets - an uneven gap, wide at the top, narrow at the bottom or narrow between two panels when compared to the other side to the vehicle will indicate some form of misalignment.
- The ability of a door, boot or bonnet to open and close without jamming or hitting its striker plate.
- Viewing along the line of the roof may show a slight dent or kink. This could indicate some serious underbody damage.

Where no visual misalignment is found, a simple test drive may reveal that the vehicle is pulling to one side. This may be due to mechanical damage to the steering or suspension, which may be the result of the vehicle hitting pot holes or striking the kerb. The use of wheel and suspension alignment equipment will reveal what damage is present.

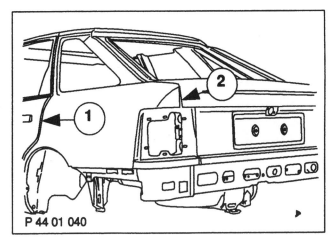

Visual check for gap and edge alignment.
1. Gap dimension. 2. Edge alignment.

If a body jig is to be used to check misalignment two main types of measuring equipment are available.

a. *The bracketless system*, which consists of the following four sub-systems:

i. An alignment bench
ii. A hydraulically-operated pull arm (draw aligner)
iii. A measuring system
iv. A comprehensive range of data sheets

With the bracketless system, the vehicle is mounted and held on to the alignment bench as described in *A4.1.5*. The alignment bench is then used to support the measurement system, also as a datum from which the measurements are taken. When the measurement system has been zeroed and centred to the vehicle, it can now be used to check alignment by measuring in three dimensions - length, breadth and height. Before misalignment can be checked you must ensure you have located the correct data sheet for the vehicle you are working on.

The principle used with a measurement system is that extension tubes with specific adapters are designed to fit into holes in the chassis or on to bolt, nut or studs on the chassis or suspension mounting points. When the slides, extension tubes and adaptations are set as described in the data sheet, they should line up with the indicated points. If they do not, then some misalignment is evident. Two methods of calculating the extent of misalignment may be adopted.

Method 1. Place the measuring system on the measurements points of the vehicle and read the difference on the corresponding scales. Compare the values obtained with those given on the data sheet and evaluate extent of damage. (*See illustration opposite*)

Method 2. Set the measuring system to the values given in the data sheet and check the extent of damage. You can now see the differences between the locations of the adapters and those of the damaged points. (*See illustration opposite*)

Many other types of body damage and misalignment can be detected using some of the special adapters. Damage to the upper body, door apertures and macpherson strut are only some of the checks that can be carried out.

b. *The bracket system.* This system is made up as follows:
- an alignment bench.
- a hydraulic operated pull arm.
- an individual set of brackets for vehicles.
- a range of data sheets.

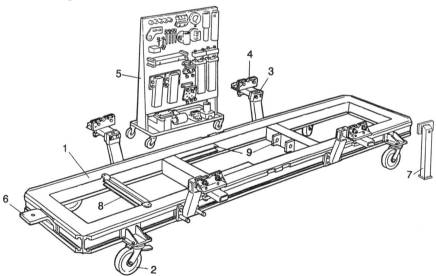

Car-O-Liner Alignment Bench detail.
1. Base frame 2. Wheels. 3. Bench mountings. 4. Chassis clamps. 5. Dolly sets. 6. Jacking plate. 7. Legs. 8. Support beam. 9. Lift attachments.

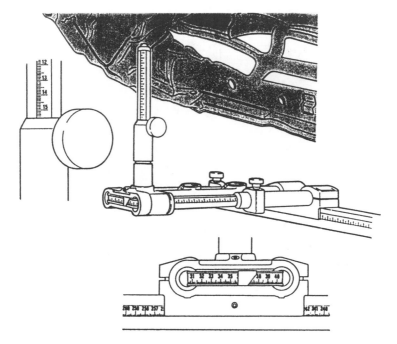

Method 1

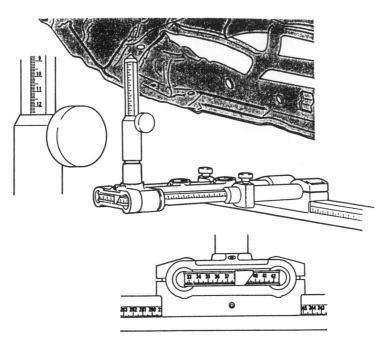

Method 2

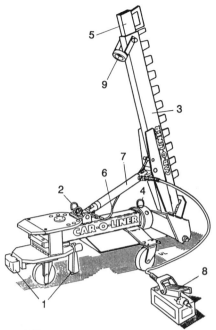

Car-O-Liner Draw Aligner
1. Locking wedge. 2. Locking peg after pivoting in sideways direction. 3.
Arm for inclining in sideways direction to give optimum pulling angle. 4.
Locking peg after inclining. 5. Extension arm. 6. Safety wire to fit
between arm and hydraulic ram mounting. 7. Hydraulic ram, 10-ton
capacity. 8. Pneumatic pump to operate hydraulic ram. 9. Mounting for
hydraulic ram.

With this system, the vehicle is attached to the alignment bench either using sill clamps or body clamps. Measurements are taken by using a set of vehicle-specific jig brackets. These brackets are bolted on to indicated areas of the underside of the vehicle. It may on occasion be required to remove some of the underside mechanical components to facilitate the jig brackets. Should a jig bracket not match up to its prescribed point on the vehicle body, this will indicate some form of misalignment. Corrective forces can be applied to realign the area until the bracket fits.

With the original jig bracket systems the jig brackets were quite large and cumbersome and were available for hire from many of the bracket hire outlets. Some bodyshops which were attached to a franchised motor dealer stocked their own bracket sets for the popular vehicles sold within the dealership. Within recent years, the jig bracket system has been modified to incorporate a set of approximately 22 universal lower brackets called *'base towers'*. A set of vehicle-specific upper brackets

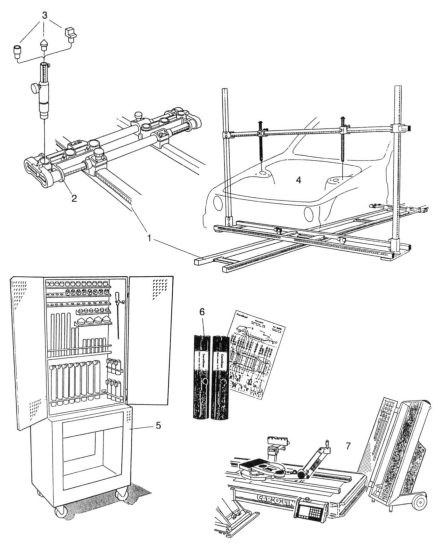

Car-O-Liner Measuring System
1. Measuring bridge. 2. Measuring slides. 3. Measuring adaptors. 4.
Measuring equipment M234 HMP. 5. Tool trolley. 6. Data sheet. 7. Car-
O-Tronic electronic measuring system.

known as *'tops'* can be fitted to the towers. The benefit of this system, such as the Celette M2 system, is that upper brackets are much smaller and lighter than the original bracket system and thus are much easier to inset or remove when the vehicle is on the bench.

The benefits of using a bracket system are that you get an immediate visual indication of any misalignment and extent of damage. The brackets

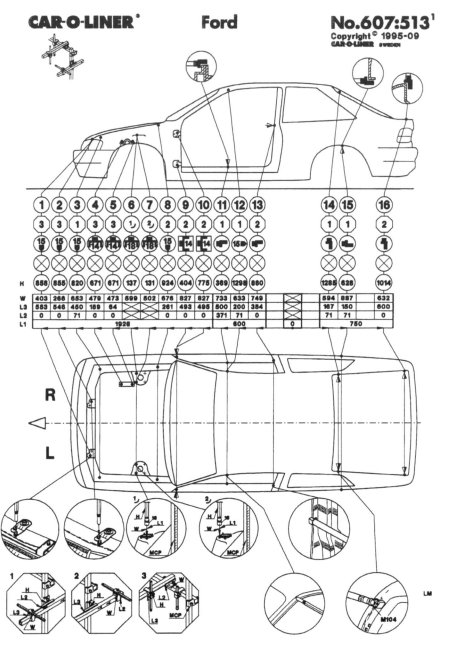

Car-O-Liner Data Sheet

can also be used as a system for clamping and welding on new parts in their exact position and also as additional clamping aids when carrying out realignment using the hydraulic push-pull unit.

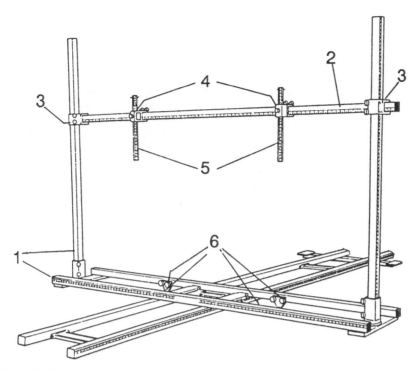

Upper body measuring equipment
1. Cross beam (1) with measuring pillars (2) **2.** Measuring bar (1). **3.** Holder L and R (2). **4.** Holders (2). **5.** Measuring rod 410 (2). **6.** Support (4).

A4.1.7   *Where appropriate, the results of measurements of vehicle alignment are recorded accurately and completely*

During the assessment of misalignment, it may be necessary to record the results of your measurements. This may be because it is a requirement for an insurance estimate or to inform the owner of the extent of damage, where the damage may render the vehicle a total loss. Either way, a systematic method of recording must be adopted.

Some jig systems, such as the Car-O-Liner 'Car-O-Tronic' system which employs a computerised system for measuring misalignment, also offer software which will record and print out a record of any misalignment found. This can be useful for customer satisfaction where a before-and-after record can be attached to the customer's vehicle service records, as well as being a useful aid for reassurance when the vehicle is resold. Blank data sheets specific to each vehicle types could also be a useful aid for recording the misalignment, which could then be used to compare against the original data sheet. (*See illustration overleaf*)

CAR-O-LINER'S CAR-O-TRONIC COMPUTER PROGRAM

1 *COS3 Main Menu: Choose what you want to do and click. Notice the "Help" icon. Click this and you'll get fast, easy-to-understand help, ideal for new users.*

2 *Repair Order: Use this screen to easily gather all information you need for repair work, i. e. customer name, vehicle make and model, insurance company, name of person doing repair work, etc.*

3 *Data Sheet Index: Here you can quickly locate the correct data sheet for the vehicle in question. Car-O-Liner's data sheets are stored on a CD-ROM disk and are updated and distributed to our subscribers four times a year.*

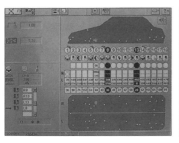

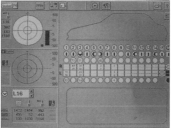

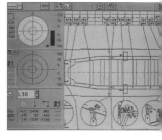

4 *Centering: Choose at least three undamaged reference points on the actual vehicle and "click" the corresponding points on the vehicle on your screen. When you've measured these points with Car-O-Tronic, centering is done.*

5 *Measurement: Measure the damaged area of the vehicle. You can now clearly see the extent of damage on your screen, represented as both a graphic illustration and a numerical value.*

6 *Data Sheet on screen: For assistance in finding reference points on the vehicle, you can at any time simply choose the detailed data sheet for the vehicle in question. You can also easily enlarge any portion of the data sheet.*

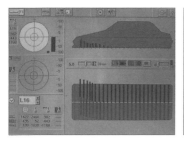

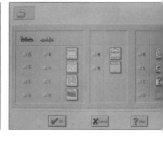

7 *Analysis: At any time during measurement work you can easily choose to see a graphic illustration of the analysis, giving a clear image of the damage. Indispensable when planning and controlling alignment work.*

8 *Pulling Control: Place the Car-O-Tronic measuring arm on a suitable reference point when preparing to pull. Several large and distinct graphic illustrations are available to assist you in steering the "pull" to a perfect result.*

9 *Print Out: At any time during a repair you can easily print out a report containing complete information on all work performed to that point.*

68

A4.1.8   Hydraulic repair equipment is prepared and attached using
approved methods

When fitting the hydraulic pull/push units safety is of utmost importance and must be strictly adhered to. All jig manufacturers will supply an instruction booklet which will describe all safety steps to take.

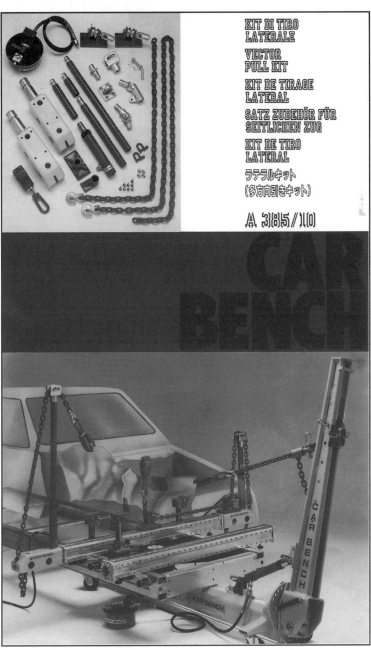

KIT DI TIRO
LATERALE

VECTOR
PULL KIT

KIT DE TIRAGE
LATERAL

SATZ ZUBEHÖR FÜR
SEITLICHEN ZUG

KIT DE TIRO
LATERAL

ラテラルキット
(多方向引きキット)

A 385/10

*Car
bench
bracket
system*

BT+A308+A296/17+C200/7+C208/4+C201/2+A7

Car bench showing universal bracket system

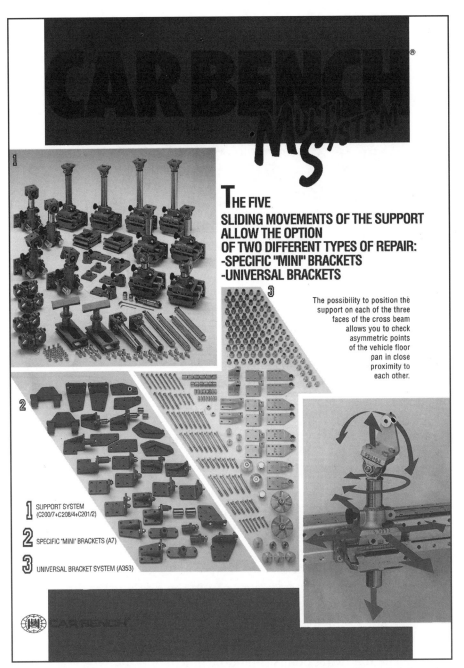

CAR BENCH®

THE FIVE SLIDING MOVEMENTS OF THE SUPPORT ALLOW THE OPTION OF TWO DIFFERENT TYPES OF REPAIR:
-SPECIFIC "MINI" BRACKETS
-UNIVERSAL BRACKETS

The possibility to position the support on each of the three faces of the cross beam allows you to check asymmetric points of the vehicle floor pan in close proximity to each other.

1 SUPPORT SYSTEM
(C200/7+C208/4+C201/2)

2 SPECIFIC "MINI" BRACKETS (A7)

3 UNIVERSAL BRACKET SYSTEM (A353)

Car bench bracket system. 1. Support system. 2. Specific mini bracket (specific to individual vehicle models). 3. Universal bracket system.

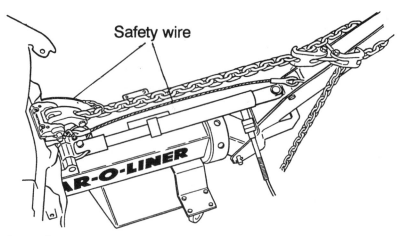

The draw aligner

With the vehicle firmly attached to the jig bench and all misalignment determined, the hydraulic pulling system can now be fitted. The illustration shown below shows how the Car-O-Liner draw aligner is attached to the alignment bench.

Most pull/push units are multi-positioned, so it is important that the pull arm is locked in the upright position prior to being moved.

IMPORTANT NOTES WHEN FITTING HYDRAULIC DRAW UNIT:

- Position the pull unit in accordance with the impact angle of damage.
- Correct positioning of the pull unit will minimise the number of times it has to be moved during the course of work.
- When a suitable anchoring angle has been determined, secure the pull unit to the bench.

To obtain maximum performance from the pull unit, and to prevent damage to it, the direction of pulling with the chain must coincide with the centre line of the hydraulic ram.

With the pull unit firmly attached to the bench it can now be prepared for use. The following points should be noted:

- Ensure that the safety cable between the pull arm and the cylinder mounting is undamaged and fitted correctly.
- Ensure that the safety cable is fitted between the vehicle and the pulling chain; this will prevent injury should the clamp loose its grip.

1. POSITIONING AND LINKING THE DRAW ALIGNER

IMPORTANT: *Make sure that the draw aligner is correctly secured to the bench frame.*

1.1

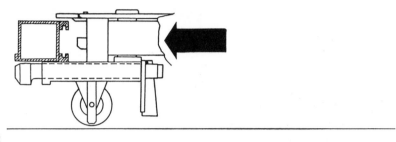

1.2

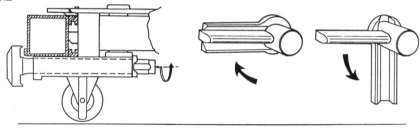

1.3

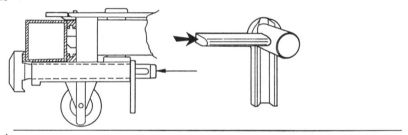

1.4

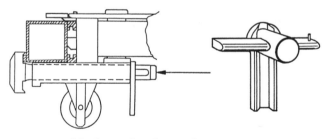

Positioning and linking the draw aligner

- Ensure no one is standing behind the pull arm.
- Clean the part of the vehicle where the pull unit will be secured; this will ensure the clamp has a good grip.
- Always use approved chain and make sure all clamps, hooks and plates are undamaged and in good condition.

- Make sure the hydraulic hose is undamaged. The hydraulic operating pressure can be as high as 600 bar (8000 psi), and the oil pressure can cause severe injury if the hose bursts.
- Ensure there is no air in the hydraulic system. Bleed the system as follows:
  - Connect the pump hose to the ram.
  - Pull the ram to the end position.
  - Hold the pump 1.5 to 2 metres above floor level then release the plunger. The compression spring will force the ram back and expel any air out of the system.
  - Repeat this procedure until all air is expelled.

A4.1.9 *Hydraulic repair equipment is operated using approved methods and techniques*

Hydraulic pulling equipment can be operated using one of two power sources - hand pump and air-operated. Whichever system you are using, you must use it in accordance with the instruction laid down in the manufacturer's operation manual. Failure to use the equipment's approved methods may cause serious damage to the equipment or injury to the operator.

Before using the hydraulic pulling equipment, and after you have determined the extent of damage, you will have to determine the direction and angles required for the corrective forces. As a general rule, any correctional forces should be in the reverse order to that which caused them, starting with the damage that has travelled furthest in the vehicle. This will prevent you overpulling the damaged area closest to the pull arm, only to find that there is damage further in which cannot be pulled later.

Two main types of pull can be made:
- A rough pull using large hooks or chains wrapped around a cross member or chassis leg. This is only carried out for rough alignment where the cross member or chassis leg is likely to be cut off and replaced.
- An accurate pull where you will make use of the clamp or special attaching arms (eg McPherson Strut pulled). During this type of pull you will be gauging you realignment with the sizes on the data sheet.

If you are using a Universal Measuring System (bracketless), you will need to lower the measuring pointer from around the damaged area. This will prevent them from being damaged by bending or twisting during the pulling operation.

The pull should be made in stages, with the power being released between each pull to allow for spring-back. Measurements should be checked each time a pull is made. It is better to make a number of small pulls rather than one large pull, which may result in the damage being over-pulled or stretched, which will make it very difficult to return it to its required dimension.

If you are using a bracket system, the bracket will not fit until the damage has been made good. The same procedure should be adopted as with the measurement system. Once the damaged area has been realigned, the bracket can be fitted and this will act as an additional aid in supporting the vehicle and also prevent that area being pulled further while you are working on or pulling another area.

Remember when using this hydraulic equipment to observe all these safety precautions:

- Any wedges, clamps or brackets are firmly secured.
- If the pull system is restrained using a wedge, always use a copper hammer when hitting the wedge.
- Make sure all safety cables are fitted.
- Make sure no one stands behind the pull-arm.
- Ensure all air and hydraulic pipes are free from cuts or fractures and are secured firmly.
- Never leave the pulling system unattended when it is under pressure.

A4.1.10 Vehicle alignment is reinstated to the manufacturers' specification and tolerances

When reinstating vehicle alignment, you will have very carefully to carry out full assessment of the extent of the damage and misalignment before you can successfully correct the damage. This assessment will normally be carried out during the measurement stages. After determining the extent of the damage, you will have to establish the direction and type of pull for reinstatement. Various clamps and pull hooks are available to assist in the pulling operation. Choose one that will be easily attached, and will remain attached, during the pull and will cause the least amount of damage to the area being pulled. During the pulling/pushing operation, make regular checks with the measuring points or brackets to ensure you are pulling in the correct direction and that you are not over-pulling the damaged areas.

Remember that, when you have pulled to the dimensions stated on the data shet, there will be a certain degree of spring-back when the tension is released. This will require the pull to be taken slightly beyond the data measurements. It is also better if you pull in stagers and make frequent checks to prevent over-pulling or pulling in the wrong direction.

The following diagrams show examples of both upper-body and under-body pulls.

continue on page 81

Alignment work

3. EXAMPLES OF TYPICAL PULLS

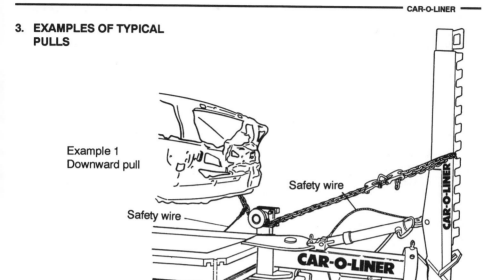

Example 1
Downward pull

Safety wire

Safety wire

CAR-O-LINER

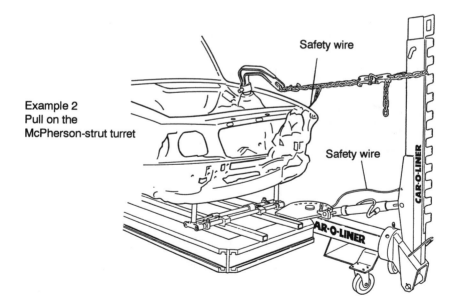

Example 2
Pull on the
McPherson-strut turret

Safety wire

Safety wire

CAR-O-LINER

Alignment work

3. EXAMPLES OF TYPICAL PULLS

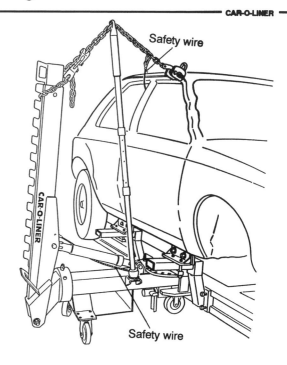

Example 3
Upward pull
at roof edge

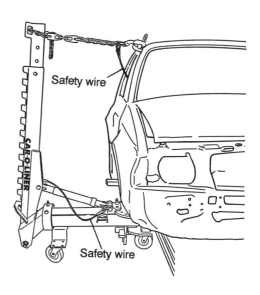

Example 4
Side pull at roof
edge with extended
draw aligner arm

Alignment work

3. EXAMPLES OF TYPICAL PULLS

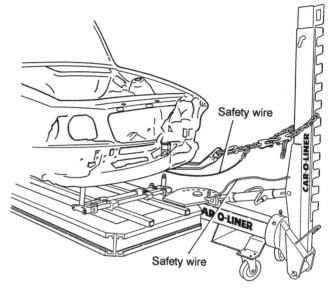

Example 5
Forward pull on
frame member

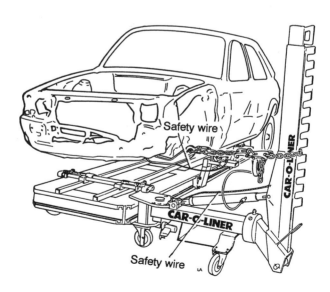

Example 6
Side pull on
frame member

Alignment work

3. EXAMPLES OF TYPICAL PULLS

Example 7
A combination of push and pull

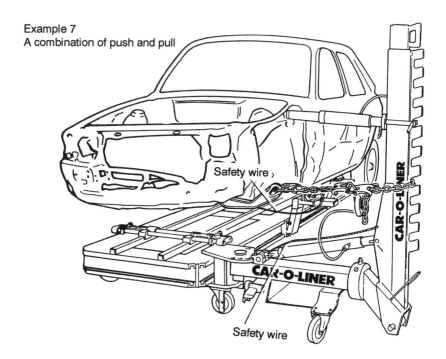

Safety wire

Safety wire

When carrying out realignment using a bracket system, brackets can be attached as each area is pulled to correct alignment. This will act as extra body restraints which will hold the specific area in place and allow other areas to be pulled without losing the correct position of the areas being clamped by the brackets.

Many jigs which have a universal measurement system have restraint dolly sets with vehicle attachment clamps and universal mountings which can be used together in a range of combinations. Measuring points which have been realigned - for example, the joint between the front axle member and the chassis side member - can be held in position by use of the dolly sets. Alignment can then be carried out on other parts of the body, without risk of losing the correct position for this point.

The components of the dolly set can also be used in conjunction with standard chassis clamp to act as extra anchoring of the vehicle to the bench.

The following diagrams show some illustrations for the use of dolly sets.

continue on page 86

Alignment work

4. USE OF DOLLY SETS

Dolly sets B63

Examples of fixing of aligned points, or added anchoring of the vehicle to the bench.

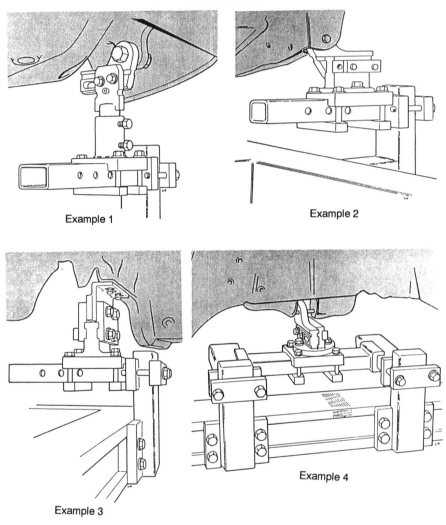

Example 1

Example 2

Example 3

Example 4

Alignment work

4. USE OF DOLLY SETS

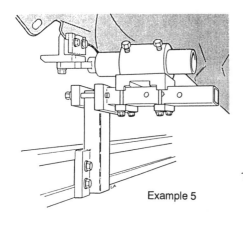

Example 5

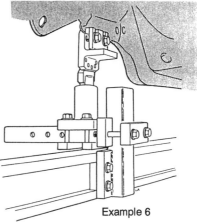

Example 6

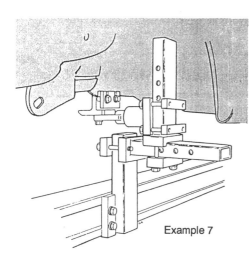

Example 7

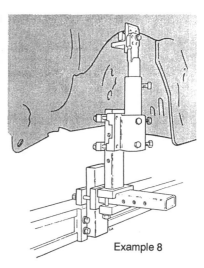

Example 8

Alignment work

4. USE OF DOLLY SETS

Dolly sets B63

Examples of use of the B63 set to apply a pull in a particular direction.

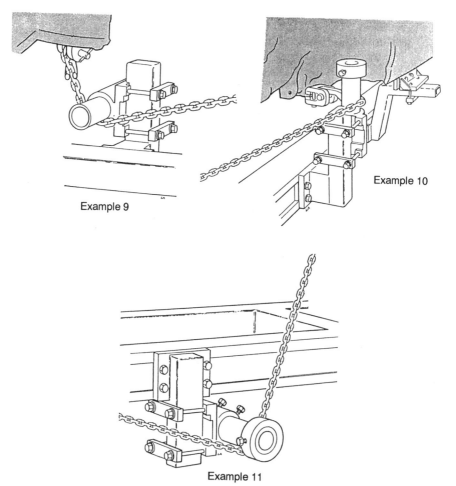

Example 9

Example 10

Example 11

Alignment work

4. USE OF DOLLY SETS

Dolly sets B64

Examples of use of B64 set for fixing points and obtaining a pull in a particular direction.

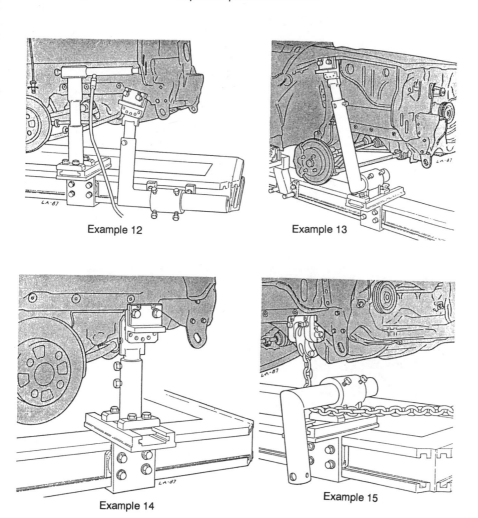

Example 12

Example 13

Example 14

Example 15

A4.1.11   Vehicle realignment is complete within approved timescales

Refer to *A2.1.7.*

A4.1.12   Where the reinstatement is likely to exceed the approved timescale, the circumstances are reported promptly to an authorised person
Refer to *A2.1.8.*

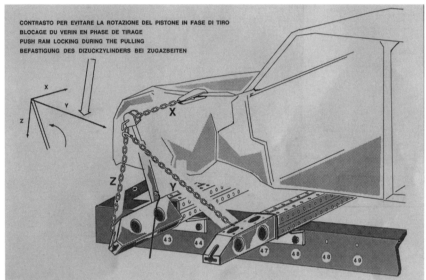

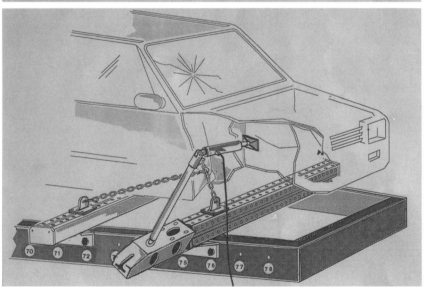

A4.1.13   *Reinstatement activities are performed in accordance with statutory and organisational policy and procedure for health and safety.*

Refer to *A2.1.9.*

A4.2 REMOVE VEHICLE BODY SECTIONS AND PREPARE SURFACES TO RECEIVE NEW SECTIONS

A4.2.1 Appropriate information is accessed from appropriate sources to inform the procedures for the removal of damaged sections

The type of damaged sections to remove in this unit will be main structured body members - that is, chassis members, body sill sections, inner wing panels, boot floor and, possibly, the main vehicle floor. In order to remove these structured panels, a great deal of stripping may be required. Not only will this be of ancillary components, it will also involve interior and exterior trim and possibly non-structured panels such as doors, boot/bonnet and wings, the procedure for which has been covered in Unit *A2* where the source of information is stated in *A2.1.1*.

A4.2.2 Protective clothing and equipment appropriate to the repair activities are used

Refer to the end chapter *A13*, to *A2.1.2* and to *A4.1.2*.

A4.2.3 Sections not subject to repair are protected, where appropriate, using approved methods and equipment

When repairing or replacing body sections, you will have to ensure you do not cause any unnecessary damage to all areas that are not subject to the repair activity. These areas will more likely be the panels adjacent to the damage. There will also be any mechanical components that cannot be removed, any glass - both on the vehicle and any within the working area - and the repair/measuring equipment.

Much of the protection you offer these areas will be common-sense measures and if you give some thought and use a planned approach you will be going a long way towards protecting the areas mentioned from damage. However, the careful use of spark covers, screen and component isolation/removal will certainly aid protection.

The use of fire-resistant blankets, fire extinguishers and water bottles will reduce the risk of damage during burning or heating within the repair area. As an extra precaution when heating, burning or welding, it is advisable to have someone to watch for you in case a fire may occur. This is especially important when you are welding, cutting or heating under the vehicle, where you are unable to see inside. Even if you have completely removed all flammable materials from around the repair area, fire is still always a hazard.

A4.2.4 Damaged sections are removed using approved methods and equipment

The type of damaged panels and sections that are dealt with in this unit are main structural sections and therefore fall into the category of *stressed* panels/sections. The basic procedures for this type of section removal has been dealt with in *A2.1.3*, but there is a major difference in that this type of panel removal may involve areas that are inaccessible and very difficult to gain access to without first removing the non-stressed panels. For example, for removal of a front inner wing you will first have to remove the wing, followed by the front panel. Damage to the inner wing will most likely have also caused damage to all the panels in front of it and you may have used the front panel area as a pulling area to gain basic body alignment. The method of panel removal will involve drilling, spot welds, burning and manual cutting, followed by dressing up the flange ready to accept the new section. Some sections, such as a single chassis leg or basic cross member (out rigger), may be damaged but will have caused no misalignment or surrounding damage. These can be easily repaired by the method mentioned above. This type of damage is typical to that caused by running over a high object such as a high kerb or stone.

A4.2.5 Damaged surfaces are restored to a condition suitable for the fitting of new sections

After you have removed all the damaged sections you will have to make good any other damage that may be evident on any other sections or panels that are not going to be replaced. Your first aim is to reinstate the areas that are to receive the new sections; then dress up all other areas using the hand tools as described previously. At this stage you may also have to use hydraulic push/pull equipment with its selection of attachments. Remember that, when using this push/pull hydraulic equipment, your anchor point, or the area you are using for the push to be taken from, must be able to support the corrective forces without causing further damage. Any hydraulic pushing or pulling should be done in stages, with the pressure released between stages to allow for spring-back and for accurate checking.

After all corrective stages have been completed the areas that have to receive the new section should be coated with a zinc-oxide weld through primer which will help reduce the formation of corrosion between the joints should moisture be present.

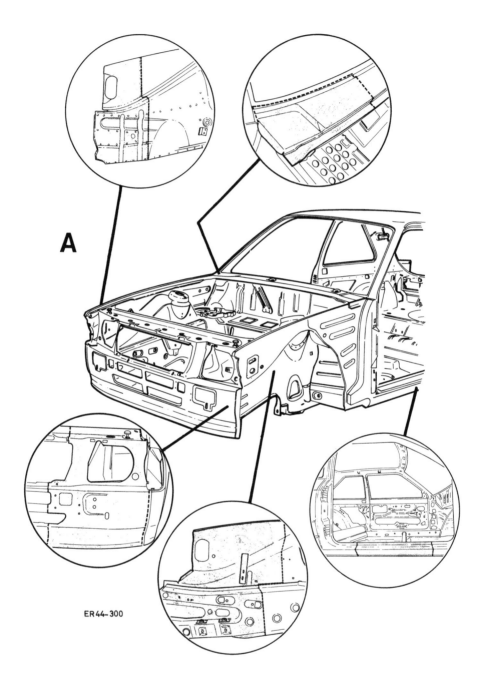

*Diagram of possible sections and part-panels that may be replaced: **A** at front of car and **B** at rear of car.*

ER44-300

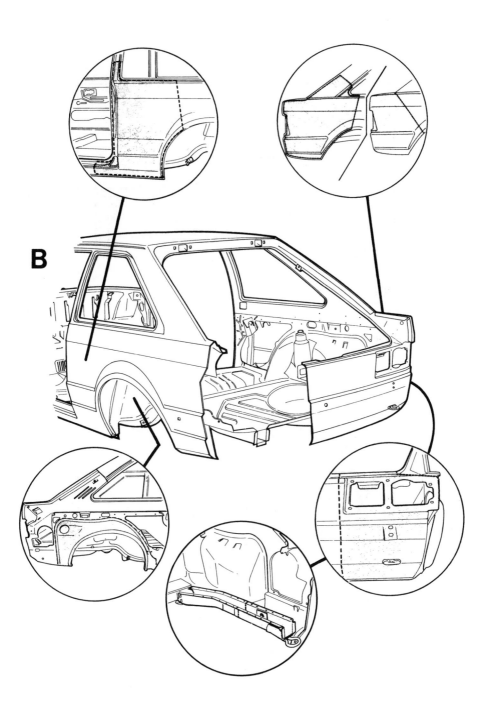

B

Examples of removal of a side member

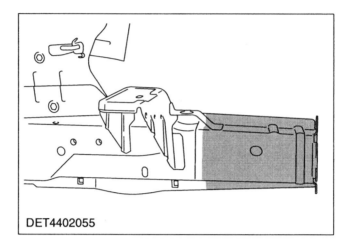

DET4402055

1. General view.

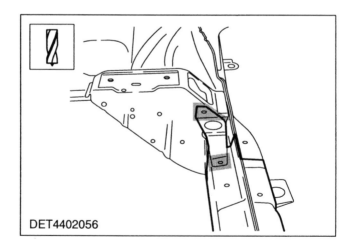

DET4402056

2. Mill out the spot welds at the air filter housing bracket and remove the old part.

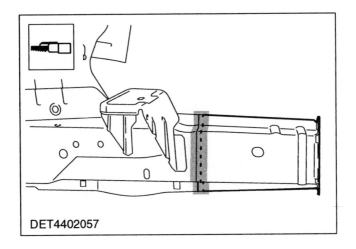

DET4402057

3. Make a rough cut. (NOTE: the cut line must be directly in front of the resistance weld seam).

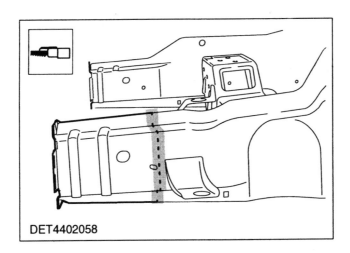

DET4402058

4. Make a rough cut at the side member flange. (NOTE: The cut line must be offset by approximately 40mm forward of the side member cut line).

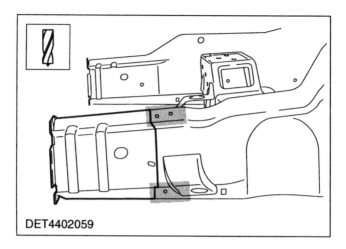

DET4402059

5. *Mill out the spot welds and remove the old part.*

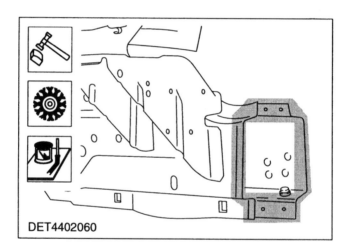

DET4402060

Preparing the old parts to receive new section

A4.2.6   *The removal of damaged sections is completed within approved timescales*
  Refer to *A2.1.7.*

A4.2.7   *Where the removal of damaged sections is likely to exceed the approved timescale, the circumstances are reported promptly to an authorised person*
     Refer to *A2.1.8.*

A4.2.8   Removal activities are performed in accordance with statutory and organisational policy and procedure for health and safety
Refer to *A2.1.9.*

A4.3 ALIGN AND FIT REPLACEMENT BODY SECTIONS

A4.3.1 Appropriate information is accessed from appropriate sources to inform the required fitting activities
Refer to *A2.1.1*.

A4.3.2 Protective clothing and equipment appropriate to the fitting activities are used
Refer to *A13, A2.1.2* and *A4.1.2*.

A4.3.3 Jig alignment fixtures are prepared and adjusted in accordance with equipment manufacturers' specification

In order to ensure an accurate fit of the replacement panels and sections, you must select and prepare the alignment equipment in accordance with the manufacturers' specification. The information required to ensure correct specification will be listed on the data sheet for the specific vehicle being repaired.

The method adopted for the alignment of the new section will depend on the type of equipment you are using in your workshop. As previously described, you will either be using a universal measurement system (bracketless) or a bracket system.

Bracketless system

In conjunction with the measurement equipment, many manufacturers of this type of jig system supply a variety of dollies and restraints which can be used as an aid to support and align the new sections to be fitted. These restraints are only fitted and used as an aid in holding the replacement section and are, therefore, only fitted when the replacement sections have been fitted in their correct position and checked, using the necessary measurement points as described in the data sheet.

Bracket system

The bracket system differs in that the vehicle alignment measurements are taken from specific brackets which are fitted in accordance with the information given on the vehicle data sheet. These brackets have a dual purpose, that of panel and section alignment and also as a restraint. The selection and preparation of these brackets will have taken place during the assessment of the damage, so it is important that the same brackets are used during the fitting of the replacement sections.

A4.3.4 *Replacement sections are aligned and secured within the tolerance specified for the particular vehicle*

When the replacement sections are being fitted, you must be aware of any tolerances that are allowed. When fitting sections that may have mechanical, steering and suspension components fitted, the tolerance may be very small. This is because any excessive allowances may result in steering and suspension misalignment which, at a later date, may have a detrimental effect on the handling and stability of the vehicle. Other areas of the unitary-constructed vehicle body will have larger tolerances, where slight variation can be taken up with panel adjustment. These areas and sections may be wings, doors, bonnet and boot/tailgates areas, where the accuracy of the fitted sections and panels may be gauged by looking at the gap between the panels and adjusting accordingly.

With the new replacement sections placed into position, they may be clamped and checked for correct alignment. Until any brackets, special clamps or restraints are fitted to the replacement sections, you may have to hold these new sections in position using tack welds or self-tapping screws. The method used to align and secure the new sections differ between the bracket system and the bracketless system as follows:

Bracketless system

- Fit the new section into position ensuring a tight fit all around its mounting points.
- Clamp section/panel in position.
- Check alignment against information shown on the data sheet.
- Adjust the section/panel until correct alignment is achieved.
- Attach any function restraints or brackets to aid in holding the sections before welding takes place.
- Any surrounding panels should now be fitted and held into position to check for overall alignment.

Once you are satisfied that all panels and sections are securely held and in correct alignment, you may remove any panels you used for alignment checking. You are now in a position to prepare for welding.

Refer back to the diagrams of the Car-O-Liner dolly sets shown with A4.1.10.

Bracket system

- Fit the new sections into position ensuring a tight fit all around the mounting points.

- Clamp sections/panels into position.
- Refit the required brackets from the special bracket kit for the specific vehicles, as described on the data sheet. This will ensure the section is in correct alignment.
- Any surrounding panels should now be fitted and held in position to check for overall alignment.

Once you are satisfied that all panels and sections are securely held and in correct alignment, you may remove any panels you used for alignment checking. You are now in a position to prepare for welding.

You are again referred to the earlier illustrations of brackets and their use in holding panels.

A4.3.5 Sections are fitted using approved methods, materials and equipment

The method used when fitting structural body sections will be welding, the type of welding depending on:
- the type of metal being welded
- the location of the welds
- the type of equipment available
- the type of joint to be made.

The main consideration to be taken when fitting the new panels and sections is that, during the repair of accident damage, your main aim is to return the vehicle to the pre-accident condition, and in doing so this will include the welding process. For example, if a panel or section was held in position during the manufacture process using spot or MAGS welding, the replacement section should also use the same process.

Before any welding takes place on the vehicle body, you must first carry out sample welds on similar metal. At this point any adjustments to the welding equipment can be made. The test weld must also be tested for strength.

CAUTION: Before any welding operation takes place the following precautions should be observed.
- Do not wear readily flammable overalls.
- Fuel lines, fuel tank and any other materials must be removed, if welding in their vicinity.
- When carrying out repair work on roof, 'A' pillar, front cross-member, rocker panels, rear wings, side panels or back panels, the wiring looms running on or between these parts must be removed or temporarily repositioned.

- Similar treatment must be given to water drain hoses located in the 'A' pillars, roof intermediate panels, 'C' pillars and between outer and inner panels on cars with sliding sunroofs.

WELDING METHODS
Oxy-acetylene (gas welding)
This method of panel joining is not recommended, due to the high stress levels during contraction and the distortion which will necessitate additional reworking in the form of straightening.

Resistance welding (spot welding)
With electric resistance welding, the parts are brought to melting point by an electric current at a point of contact between two copper electrodes and fused together by pressure. All the points to be welded must be accessible with the various electrode arms available.

MAGS welding (Metal, Arc, Gas Shielded)
With this method, an automatically-fed welding rod (electrode) is fused under a veil of inert gas. The weld melts before the oxygen (air) can get at it. The main advantages of MAGS welding are the minimised contraction stresses and distortion. Because very little heat is generated during welding, surrounding heat-sensitive parts often may not need to be removed. With this method, overlapping panels can be joined together from one side by puddle welding (a hole is drilled on the top panel and the weld is filled from the bottom panel to the top through this hole.)

Butt joints can also be carried out provided a very small gap is present and the weld is staggered throughout its length.

REPAIR PROCEDURE
Of the welding methods described, the main one used for body work repair is resistance spot welding.

Satisfactory spot-welded joints can only be obtained by observing the following points:
- Closeness of contact between the two or more panels or flanges.
- Contact pressure of the electrode areas.
- Always use the shortest electrodes possible.
- Panel joints must be cleaned down to bare metal by removing any traces of paint, rust, grease or oil.

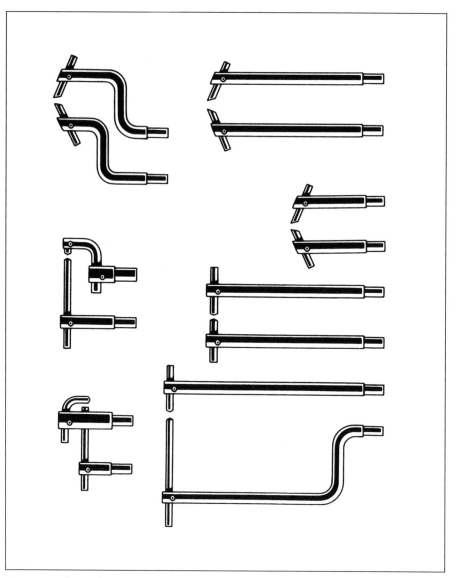

Various eletrode set-ups

- Apply a suitable zinc-rich welded-through rust preventative primer before welding.
- The welding current.
- The size/diameter and the spacing of the spot welds. The spot welds should be at least 3.5 mm in diameter.
- The gap between any two spot welds should be between 25 and 35 mm. You should try to use factory spacing where possible.

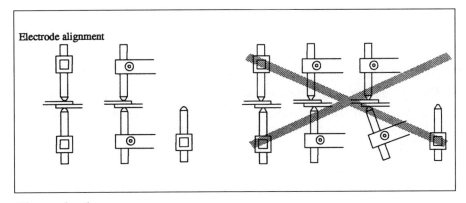

Electrode alignment

Any weld seams or spots should always lie in the middle of the panel edges or flanges.

SPOT WELD TESTING

Welds must be shear-tested with a thin chisel or screw driver to check minimum shear strength, which will depend upon the thickness of the metal.

The spot welds will be regarded as satisfactory if the panel does not pull away at the welds during the shear test. The chisel is slid into the gaps between the welded panels at a number of points and moved gently to and fro.

A weld is defective if there are any signs of burning, porosity or cracking.

Any defective spot welds found should be drilled out and the panel should be joined together using a MAGS plug weld.

A4.3.6 *Sealants are selected and applied according to the manufacturers' specification for type, method of application and thickness*

The factors which influence the selection and application methods of a sealer will depend upon:

The types of joints to be sealed. These could be: between panel joints, as gap fillers between panels, or drip checks on gutters.

The elements to be sealed against. Sealers are available in various compositions and viscosities. Panel joints are sealed to prevent the ingress of water, whereas a gap filler will also hold out road dirt, mud etc, as well as wind and draughts. Sealers will also be used on the complete underbody to prevent corrosion, damage from stone chips and general abrasion. When sealer is applied to complete panels, this will also help reduce panel drum and vibration and help in general sound deadening.

The equipment available for sealer applications. Sealers can be applied by various methods: brush, spray, cartridge, sealer gun or spreading knife. When applying sealers it is desirable to have the finish on the applied sealer similar to that of the factory finish.

Many vehicle manufacturers will specify types of sealers to be used around the vehicle and may list three or four different types. These may be supplied as a part using the manufacturer's part number. Where there are no sealers available from the manufacturer, there will be a recommendation; that is, a vehicle manufacturer may allow you to use a sealer supplied by 3M or Sikaflex, provided they are used and applied in accordance with the instruction supplied.

Companies such a 3M, Sikaflex and Tereson produce a variety of sealers for most appliances.

The following list gives examples of the types of sealers available:

Sprayable under-body sealer (Schutz) and stone-chip materials
Polyurethane adhesive sealers
Acrylic joint-sealing compound
Silicone adhesive sealing compounds
Drip-check sealer
Body caulking
Weld-through sealer

The different materials can only adhere properly and ensure long-term protection when applied to a clean dry surface.

The main properties of a good sealing compound are that it has good adhesion, remains flexible without cracking and can be over painted.

CAUTION. As with all chemical compounds they must be used with caution and all safety precautions observed.

- Apply in a well-ventilated area.
- Wear suitable mask when spraying.
- Wear clear goggles, rubber gloves and overalls.
- Cover up all areas not requiring sealing.

A4.3.7 The alignment and refitting of sections is completed within approved timescales
Refer to *A2.1.7.*

A4.3.8 *Where the alignment and refitting of sections is likely to exceed the approved timescales, the circumstances are reported promptly to an authorised person*
    Refer to *A2.1.8.*

A4.3.9 *Fitting activities are performed in accordance with statutory and organisational policy and procedure for health and safety*
    Refer to *A2.1.9.*

A4LH   UNDERPINNING KNOWLEDGE

RECTIFY CHASSIS FRAME MISALIGNMENT AND REPAIR/REPLACE CHASSIS SECTIONS

A4.1   REINSTATE CHASSIS FRAME ALIGNMENT

A4.1.1   Appropriate information is accessed from appropriate sources to inform the procedures for the reinstatement of alignment

As this unit covers vehicles which have separate chassis frames, the information sources will be limited to those supplied by the vehicle manufacturer. Typical examples of vehicles covered within this unit will be light and heavy vehicles with coach-built bodies, small and large passenger-carrying vehicles with separate chassis, and saloon vehicles produced in low quantity, which may be either kit cars or cars which have glass reinforced plastic (GRP) bodies. All of these vehicles are fitted with bodies which can be unbolted from the chassis. The commercial body builder or kit-car manufacturer will have chassis diagrams showing dimensions and mounting points. The main vehicle (chassis/cab) manu-facturers will also have details of dimensions for their vehicles. For some of the more popular vehicles, details may be available from some of the alignment equipment manufacturers, such as Black Hawk, Car-O-Liner, Josam, Cellette etc. With extensive body and chassis damage, details for both the body and chassis dimensions may be required. Manufacturers of body or chassis alignment and straightening equipment may produce a comprehensive instruction manual which will give a description and application of all components and accessories, before going on to show examples of repair situations and corrective procedures.

A4.1.2   Protective clothing and equipment appropriate to the repair activities are used

Refer to Unit *A13* and *A2.1.2* for general awareness.

Vehicles with separate chassis construction differ from unitary constructed vehicles in that they are usually much heavier, with weights ranging from 2 tons to 40 tons. Because of this wide weight range specialist lifting equipment may be required. The average hydraulic trolley jack will not be sufficient to raise one of these vehicles. Therefore, you must check that the SWL of the trolley jack is greater than the weight of the vehicle being lifted. Care should be taken when supporting large vehicles, whether on a jack or axle stands, that no unnecessary stress is placed on the chassis so as to support it out of alignment. An example of this would be a support placed under an outrigger at one side of the chassis and another placed under a chassis main runner on the other side. When large vehicles are raised above the ground, the stress placed on the chassis should be the same as that which is caused when the vehicle is on its wheels.

A4.1.3 Equipment selected for the assessment of vehicle alignment is appropriate to the vehicle manufacturers' specification

For general information refer to *A4.1.3* (Unitary Construction). In the case of low-production, hand-built or kit cars, no data sheets may be available from any of the sources previously mentioned. Nevertheless, the equipment you select may be quite simple. It could range from trammels, gun-sight gauges or a drop-line check. Although this type of vehicle may be rare in your workshop, you should still be able to cater for this type of repair. Extensive damage to the chassis of a separate-constructed vehicle may be more evident. As the chassis is bolted to the body, you may find no body misalignment, but the chassis could be bent and could have pulled the mounting points from the body. Where the body has also misaligned, visual inspection will show the degree of misalignment evident.

With heavy commercial vehicles, buses and trailers, alignment equipment is available which enables you to measure any misalignment in the chassis, between axles and wheels. Although this type of equipment is only used within the commercial vehicle sector of the motor industry, companies such as Josam supply laser measuring equipment.

A4.1.4 Equipment used for the assessment of vehicle alignment is prepared and adjusted in accordance with the equipment manufacturers' specifications

Refer to *A4.1.4* (Unitary Construction).

A4.1.5 The vehicle is prepared and, where appropriate, installed/located on the alignment equipment in accordance with the equipment manufacturers' specification

Due to the large size and weight of many large commercial vehicles and buses, it is more likely that the alignment equipment is taken to and attached to the vehicle frame, rather than having the vehicle mounted on to it. With light commercial vehicles, by the use of special attachment clamps they may be mounted on to the same type of body jig as used for passenger cars. Special alignment jigs are available for checking alignment and repair of truck cabs, an illustration of which is shown.

With some alignment equipment, the main system consist of 'I beams' which are cast into the workshop floor. This allows work to be done free from unnecessary ramps and, furthermore, the workshop can be used for other tasks than frame and body straightening. Press/pull trolleys, frames press and other equipment is anchored to the floor beams.

Heavy girders cast along the top of a service pit can also be used, in conjunction with a moveable supporting base, to form a track for the anchorage of the frame press. The supporting bases serve as a foundation for the special jack and allow for a chain attachment by means of built-in wheels.

Examples of frame straightening are shown in the first illustration, using the JOSAM push/pull trolley system with the I beams set into the floor. The examples which follow detail practical application of the Blackhawk Power-Cage.

A4.1.6   *The nature and extent of misalignment is determined using approved methods*

When selecting and using equipment to determine the extent of misalignment, the severity of the damage will determine the equipment you will use. A visual inspection may show that there is no apparent structural damage, so you may be able to carry out your assessment using fairly basic tools, such as a tape rule, trammels or gun-sight gauges.

Typical visual checks you could do:
- Check distance between centres of wheels on each side (a simple piece of string or cord could do this).
- Check for uneven gap between the body and chassis all around the vehicle.
- Look along length of chassis and check for parallel between main chassis runners or between each chassis cross member.

With light commercial vehicles, small- and medium- panel vans, you will be able to determine the extent of damage using your measurement or bracket jig system as previously detailed in *A4:1:6* (Unitary Construction).

106

JO AV FH12-16 Adaptersats VOLVO FH12-FH16 Lång
JO AV FH12-16 Adaptersatz VOLVO FH12-FH16 Lang
JO AV FH12-16 Adapter set VOLVO FH12-FH16 Long

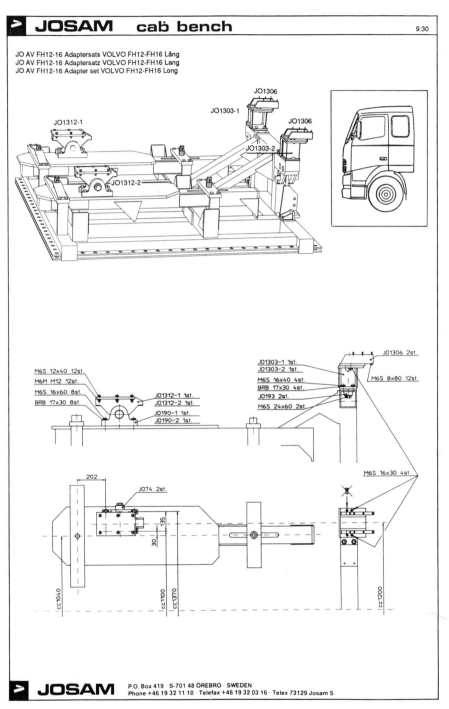

The Josam Cab Bench

107

Frame and accessories

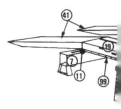

Part No.	Item	Description	Qty
ACE 1430.900.B	1	Safety catcher for item 48	1
ACE 3069.242	2	Anchor bolt M 16 × 145 (floor)*	12
ACE 3079.061 A	3	Removable pin L = 140	20
ACE 3088.108 A	72	Washer Ø46 × 92 × 6 mm for items 78, 79, 80*	12
AEK 303	4	Alloy chain (10 T)	4
AHD 00003	5	Ram adapter attached to bottom of item 42	10
AHD 00046	6	Front support and legs (includes items 14 and 15)	1
AHD 00048	7	Rear and center support	2
AHD 00049	8	Transverse beam	4
AHD 00062	9	Fulcrum bar collar	4
AHD 00068	10	Pillar bracket for item 37	4
AHD 00074	11	Main beam stop	12
AHD 80054	12	Chassis puller	4
AHD 80057	13	High pull tensioner socket	10
AHD 80064	14	Front support base	2
AHD 80069	15	Front support (without legs)	1
AHD 80070	16	Main beam C (left rear)	1
AHD 80071	17	Main beam B (left front)	1
AHD 80072	18	Main beam A (right front)	1
AHD 80073	19	Main beam D (right rear)	1
AHD 80077	20	End tower support (right)	1
AHD 80079	21	Tower	10
AHD 80083	22	Pin L = 190	30
AHD 80086	78	End roller carriage	2
AHD 80088	79	Transverse slide assembly with double row cylindrical bearings for item 8	8
AHD 80142	80	End tower slide assembly with double row conical bearings	2
AHD 80197	23	Winch and bracket assembly for item 35	1
AHD 80199	24	End tower support (left)	1
AHD 80360	82	Pin for mounting, item 23 to item 35	1
S 900 A 046	31	Hose extension (6 m) with 2 male couplers for item 30	1
S 900 A 047	32	Hose extension (6 m) with male and female coupler for item 30	1
MNLF 1450	92	Nut M 45 for items 78, 79, 80*	12
HD 408 A	34	Chain roller	20
HD 414	35	Tower extension	4
HD 414 H			2
HD 415	36	Anchor rail	1
HD 418	37	Fulcrum bar	4
HD 425 A	38	Roller block	2
HD 428	39	Main beam clamp (for assembly of items 16, 17, 18, 19 to item 7)	4
HD 437	40	Diagonal support (L'beam)	1
HD 445	41	Ramp with bolts (pair) (optional)	1
HD 451 A	42	Chain lock head (for pulls)	2
HD 453	43	Anchor chain with 2 hooks (20 T)	1
HD 3006	44	Wedge for item 45	4
HD 4751	45	Frame hook	2
HD 4950	46	Bolt package	1
K 178.264	47	Chain lock head	4
HD 452	49	Alloy chain with 1 hook (20 T)	10
Z 220	50	C frame press (20 T)	1
Z 239	51	Extension tube (250 mm) for item 48	1
Z 241	52	Extension tube (710 mm) for item 48	1
Z 242	53	Female coupling for items 51 and 52	3
Z 243	54	Ram base, item 48	1
Z 436	55	Serrated saddle	2
Z 607	56	Plunger base (for broad support)	1
Z 669	57	Male connector (for connection of different extensions on the rams)	1
Z 1041	58	Extension tube (75 mm) for item 48	1
Z 1042	59	Extension tube (125 mm) for item 48	1
Z 1043	60	Extension tube (450 mm) for item 48	1
Z 1046	61	Wedge head (for pulls)	1
Z 1047	62	Vee head	1
HD 3074	63	Accessory for indirect pushing	2
65651	64	Chain tensioner	4
95307	65	Frame guage set	4
95312	66	Tracking gauge (7.5 m)	1
95 411 A	67	Ram chain head	10

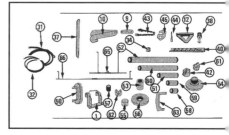

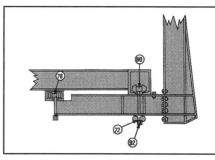

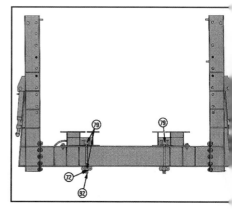

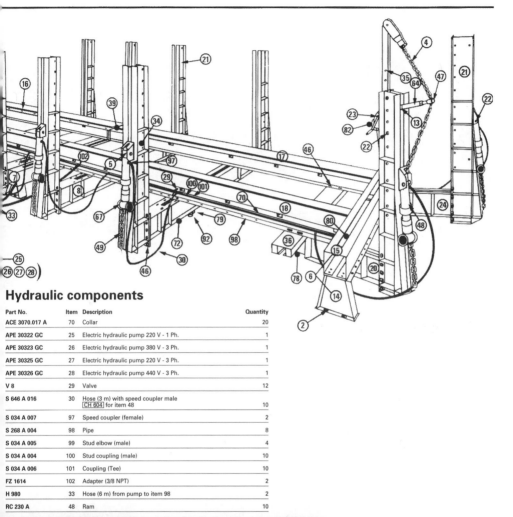

Hydraulic components

Part No.	Item	Description	Quantity
ACE 3070.017 A	70	Collar	20
APE 30322 GC	25	Electric hydraulic pump 220 V - 1 Ph.	1
APE 30323 GC	26	Electric hydraulic pump 380 V - 3 Ph.	1
APE 30325 GC	27	Electric hydraulic pump 220 V - 3 Ph.	1
APE 30326 GC	28	Electric hydraulic pump 440 V - 3 Ph.	1
V 8	29	Valve	12
S 646 A 016	30	Hose (3 m) with speed coupler male CH 604 for item 48	10
S 034 A 007	97	Speed coupler (female)	2
S 268 A 004	98	Pipe	8
S 034 A 005	99	Stud elbow (male)	4
S 034 A 004	100	Stud coupling (male)	10
S 034 A 006	101	Coupling (Tee)	10
FZ 1614	102	Adapter (3/8 NPT)	2
H 980	33	Hose (6 m) from pump to item 98	2
RC 230 A	48	Ram	10

POWER-CAGE

Re-align the chassis almost as fast as it was damaged

The damaged chassis is anchored to the pulling towers. The anchoring and straightening forces are spread and controlled by the pivot arms.

Actuation of multiple rams by hydraulic valves. Remote control of electro/hydraulic pump with hand-held control unit. The different control buttons enable accurate force adjustment.

Standard tower extension assemblies enable you to pull approximately 3.48 m above the runway and high tower extension assemblies up to 4.30 m. This is ideal for repairing cab, bus and container damage.

POWER-CAGE simplifies lateral anchoring pulling of twisted chassis, straightening of cabs... without moving the vehicle.

Ten pulling towers can be moved and positioned easily due to the use of ball bearing slide assemblies which roll along the main beam.

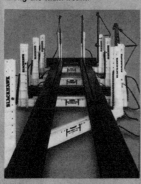

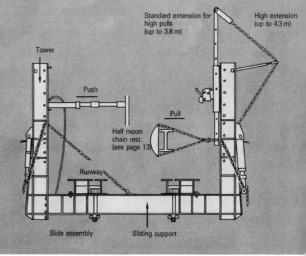

Tower

Standard extension for high pulls (up to 3.8 m)

High extension (up to 4.3 m)

Push

Pull

Half moon chain rest (see page 13)

Runway

Slide assembly

Sliding support

110

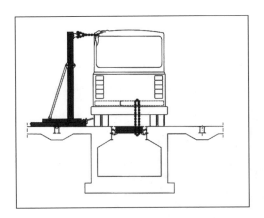

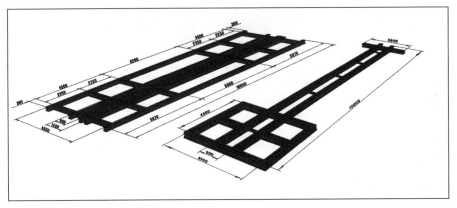

Example of floor beams and service pit (Josam)

We will now concentrate on the type of damage that can occur on a heavy truck or bus chassis which has a ladder configuration.

Before looking for misalignment, you should be aware of the type of damage that can occur to this type of vehicle. Often a description of how the damage was caused may help in determining how it is to be repaired. This is important with commercial vehicles, because not all misalignment or damage is caused by impact collision. It may be caused by using the vehicle extensively on uneven ground such as quarries or building sites, by uneven or unsecured loads, or by overloading.

Main Types Of Deformation

The main types of permanent damage to a commercial vehicle chassis are shown below. However, you may find that the damage will consist of two or more of these types of deformation.

111

The frame aligning set JO 20 consists mainly of three trolleys, JO20 AL, each with its own 20 ton hydraulic cylinder. If one press is used as a pressure tool at a 20 ton capacity, the two counterstay presses will each carry a ten ton load.

The frame aligning set JO 20-40 consists of one SR1 press with two 20 ton hydraulic cylinders which give a total press capacity of 40 tons. In addition, there are two JO 20 AL presses which provide a 20 ton press capacity.

Sidesway

A sidesway is the most common type of damage. It is usually caused by lateral forces. A diamond force may also be the source of a sidesway.

If a side rail is bent vertically it is quite probable it is also bent sideways.

As a rule, a sidesway causes some of the cross members to be displaced from right angles. The gusset of the cross members are then distorted in the same way as for a diamond displacement.

Vertical Bends, Humps And Sags

A vertical bend, hump or sag may be caused by vertical forces. A twisting force may also cause a vertical bend. Often a vertical bent frame

112

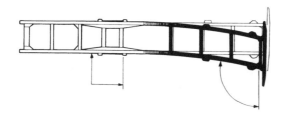

Sidesway

Bend, hump or sag

looks twisted. It is important to establish whether a frame is twisted as well as bent vertically. If it is twisted, the vertical bend has to be aligned before the twist.

Twist

A frame is twisted if the side rolls are straight but not parallel. The crossmembers furthest from the centre of the twist (the one at the front of the vehicle and the one at the rear of the vehicle) are exposed to the heaviest loads and are often distorted.

The crossmembers at the centre of a twisted chassis are exposed to torsional damage. If the crossmembers are made the same as the side rails, open section, these sections give way to twisting without great resistance and therefore do not become permanently distorted by the twist.

If the crossmembers are made of a box section, they will offer greater resistance to the twisting force, and so they may become permanently distorted or cracked by the twisting force.

Diamond Displacement

Diamond displacement is when one of the side rails is either pushed back or forward. With this type of displacement, all crossmembers will be pushed out of right angles. A typical cause of diamond displacement may be when a tipper truck trailer turns over when unloading. On trucks or trailers with diamond-ly rigid bodywork, as well as trucks with two rear axles, diamond displacement is unlikely. The same accident would instead produce a sidesway displacement.

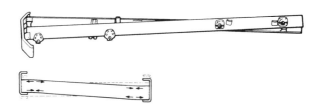

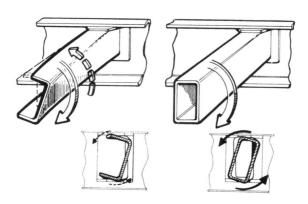

Twist

Local Damage

Local damage can be caused to any part of the chassis or frame and must be carefully checked to ensure it has not travelled further than you have seen.

Frame Gauges

The use of frame gauges suspended from the chassis will give an accurate indication of any misalignment. These gauges may require the line of sight or may include a laser beam projected from front to rear. This beam should touch each measurement point along the length of the area being checked. If the laser beam is either inside or outside the measurement point, this may indicate a sidesway. If the beam is above or below the measurement point this may show a twist or sag on the frame.

When setting up the frame gauges, it is important to ensure the vertical height of the gauges used is equal, the same applies to the horizontal sizes.

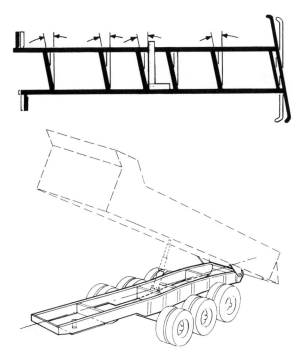

Diamond displacement (top), a deformation more common to the tipper truck (below).

An example of determining the extent of frame damage using the Josam laser system is described opposite.

After measurements have been taken, any deviation beyond a quarter of an inch (6mm) will require realignment.

If a laser projector is not available it is possible to use a tight string by the side of the sighting pins of the frame gauges.

Vertical Bends, Humps And Sags

The vertical bends of the two side rails must be measured individually.

1. Block up the chassis on two points under the front and two points under the rear to make the ends of the chassis horizontal. Use a spirit level across the chassis side rails.

2. Hang five frame gauges evenly spaced along the complete chassis. Tighten the measuring string under the frame gauges along the length of one side rail.

Sidesway

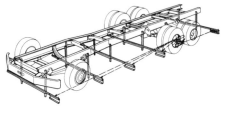

1. Hang frame gauges along frame as illustrated. If the width of the frame is different at the front and rear, one should be hung where the frame starts to taper and one where it stops tapering.

2. Attach the laser projectorto one of the wheels. Hang the measuring scales on the sighting pins of the frame gauges.

3. Adjust the laser projector so that the beam indicates the same value on the front and rear scales.

4. Point the beam at the other scales and read off the values. Make a note of all measured values.

Note: The string must be pulled extremely tight so that the sag does not affect the measuring result. The distance between the string and the frame gauge should be equal at the front and at the rear.

3. Measure the distance to the string from each of the three remaining frame gauges. Make a note of all measured values.

Measure the other side rail in the same way.

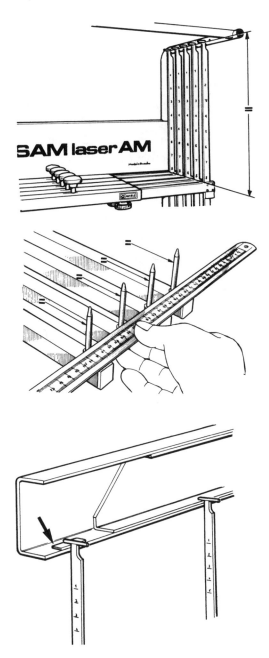

Top: *measuring with laser (avoid pointing laser at anyone's face or looking directly into the projector). Centre: Frame gauges. It is possible to adjust or check positions of sighting pins and height of frame gauges when hanging on the carriage. Bottom: Compensate for the thickness of the inner frame with spacers.*

A quick check for a vertical bend may be made without using the frame gauges and measuring string.

Using a spirit level, place it across the frame between the two side rails. The frame should be horizontal both at the front and rear. Now make similar checks along the length of the chassis frame. If the frame proves to be horizontal along its length, it is very likely that the frame has not sustained a vertical bend. This is based on the assumption that it is unlikely that both side rails are bent equally.

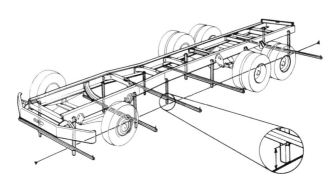

Permitted deviation will be: 1/4 inch (6mm) for each side rail; 1/8 inch (3mm) difference between the side rails. Any deviation greater than this should be rectified.

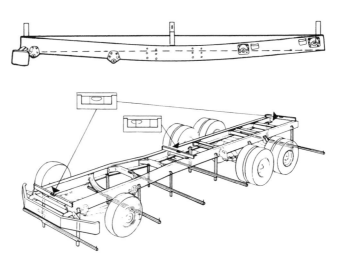

Using a spirit level placed on each crossmember as a quick check for bends, humps or sags.

Twist Damage

1. Block up the frame until it is horizontal under two points at the rear.
2. Lift the frame at the front with two hydraulic cylinders placed under the side rails and connected to the same pump. Lift until the springs are unloaded.
3. Hang a frame gauge at the front or lay the spirit level across the front of the chassis.
4. Measure how much the frame gauge deviates from the horizontal. A practical way is to use a 3ft (one metre) long spirit level. One end of the spirit level can be packed up until it is horizontal (using a twist drill as packer will give an accurate measurement, so a good selection of twist drills should be at hand).

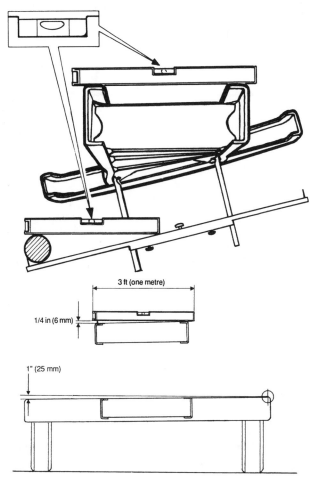

Checking for twist damage

Permitted deviation will be: 1/4 inch (6mm) per 3ft (one metre). This deviation is permissible providing that the cab or body work does not lean more than 3/8 inch (10mm) per 3ft (one metre) with the truck standing with all wheels on a level floor. The overall tilt must not exceed 1 inch (25 mm) measured from the bumper ends to the floor or body work to the floor.

Uneven springs can be the reason for the chassis frame to look twisted.

Diamond Displacement

If a frame has sustained a diamond displacement, all the crossmembers will no longer be at 90° to the side rails. The easiest method to check for diamond displacement is with the use of a set square; alternatively a template with 90° angle could also be used.

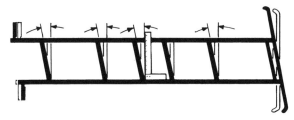

Checking the diamond displacement

Local Damage

Local damage may be apparent on a crossmember or side rail without causing any misalignment. Nevertheless, all traces of local damage should be measured and rectified.

To determine the extent of local damage, place a ruler or straight edge across the damaged area, measure the distance between the edge of ruler and the damaged member. Cracks or flaking paint may be an indication that there is a stretching of the metal underneath.

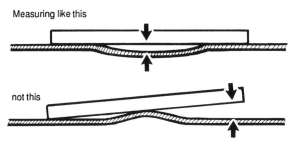

Checking local damage

A4.1.7   Where appropriate, the results of measurements of vehicle
         alignment are recorded accurately and completely

For light commercial vehicles, such as Land Rover etc, refer to *A4.1.7* (Unitary Construction).

For heavy commercial vehicles and buses, all traces of misalignment must be recorded on an appropriate form, an example of which is shown in following illustrations. This may be a requirement of the Department of Transport (DOT), as the legislation covering maintenance and road worthiness of this class of vehicle is very strict. All transport and bus operations are required to keep a file on each of their vehicles. Also, because of the size of these vehicles, a record of any deviation can be used as a reference when planning the sequence for the rectification of the damage.

A4.1.8   Hydraulic repair equipment is prepared and attached using
         approved methods

For general information on the preparation of hydraulic equipment refer to *A4.1.8* (Unitary Construction).

One of the main differences you will find when working on heavy chassis frames is that most of the corrective forces will be applied using high pressure jacks and anchors up to 40 tons. Chains may occasionally be used to aid in the restraint and anchoring of the chassis or bodywork. The illustration below shows an example of a chassis frame being prepared, and the location of press trolley jacks and anchorage trolley.

Where the press trolleys are used in conjunction with an 'I' frame cast into the floor, there must be a locking device on each side of the trolley.

A4.1.9   Hydraulic repair equipment is operated using approved
         methods and techniques

As a general guide refer to *A4.1.9* (Unitary Construction).

If you are unsure of the operating methods of any item of hydraulic equipment, it is important to gain all the information you require before

(*Text continues on page 124*)

JOSAM ©
Box 419 · S-701 48 ÖREBRO · SWEDEN

Reg. n° _ _ _ _ _ _ Type _ _ _ _ _ _ _ _ _ _ _ _ _ _ _ _
Date _ _ _ _ _ _ _ Name _ _ _ _ _ _ _ _ _ _ _ _ _ _ _ _
Miles/Km _ _ _ _ _ _ Sign _ _ _ _ _ _ _ _ _ _ _ _ _ _ _

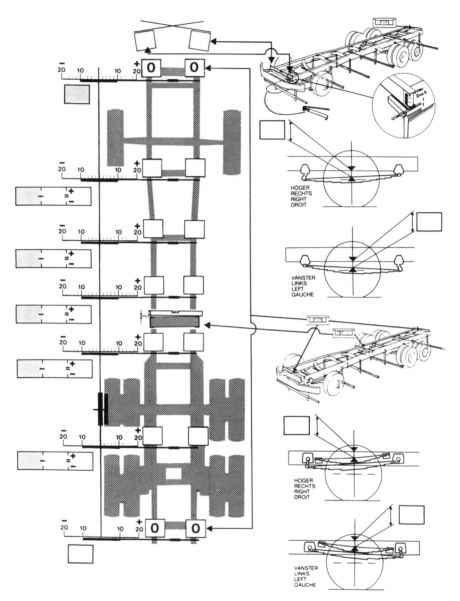

Example of sheets to record misalignments in heavy commercial vehicles

122

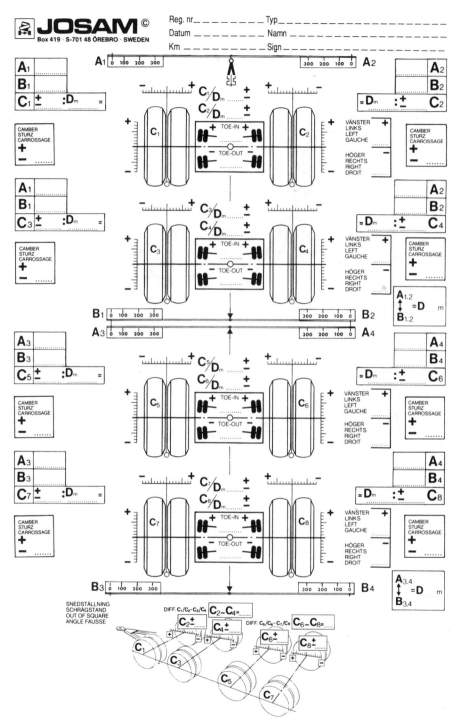

Example of sheets to record misalignments in heavy commercial vehicles

Press trolley, Trolley for anchorage

Place locking devices nearest the end where the force tries to lift the trolley. There must be a locking device on each side of the trolley.

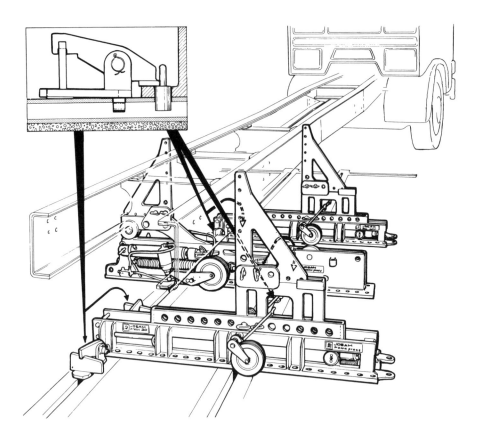

you start. All hydraulic equipment manufacturers supply a comprehensive instruction manual to aid in your understanding of their equipment. They may also provide a telephone or facsimile hotline if you require further information.

*A4.1.10   Vehicle alignment is reinstated to the manufacturers'
            specifications and tolerances*

A work sequence is very important if you require to carry out the alignment reinstatement successfully. The reinstatement sequence should be in reverse to the forces that caused the damage.

- You will have previously established the extent of damage and confirmed any local damage before you start realignment.

- Frame and body components have to be checked carefully regarding strains and cracks.
- Cracks in the paint and flaking paint are clear signs of strains in the material below.
- Check crossmembers and bodywork attachments carefully.

Due to the cross-sectional shape of the crossmember and side rails, there is a danger of the flanges deforming when either carrying out the alignment or restraining the chassis frame. To prevent this from happening, it will be necessary to put protective spacers within the crossmember. Examples of spacers are shown here.

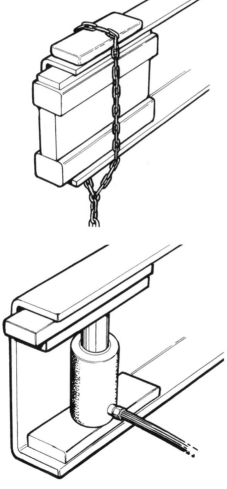

A spacer can be made using a hydraulic cylinder with small protective spacers

Aligning Force Points

- Apply the two outer of the three forces as far as possible from each other at the extreme end of the damaged area.
- Apply the middle retention or press force at the centre point between the two outer forces.

If this procedure is not followed, there is a danger of poor alignment or damage to the anchorage devices.

The examples shown presuppose that the three trolleys are at equal distances from each other. If the distances differ the result will be abnormal and unbalanced leverage.

Alignment of different types of damage

If the chassis frame has sustained more than one type of damage you should start aligning where the damage is the greatest. Often it is better to align sideways before vertical bends. All local damage should be aligned at the same time as the major damage is being aligned.

The following seven pages give examples of frame damage and realignment procedures using the 'Josam' frame repair system.

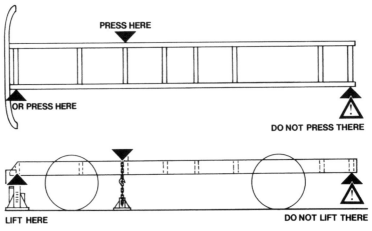

Basic principles of frame realignment

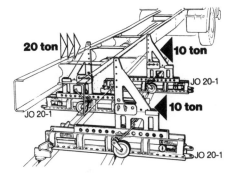

Frame aligning set JO20-BS, contains three JO20-1 trolleys with one 20 ton press capacity hydraulic cylinder each. If one trolley is used as pressure tool at a 20 ton pressure, the two counterstay trolleys each will carry a 10 ton load, provided all trolleys are at equal distances from each other.

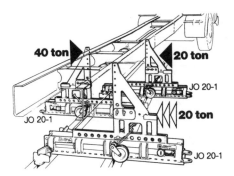

A single JO20-1 trolley may be used as a counterstay if the hydraulic cylinder works mechanically in bottom position. It will then carry 40 tons of pressure power through leverage when its twin trolley presses 20 tons. Observe! The hydraulic cylinder must be fully retracted. Otherwise it may take more pressure than it has been designed for.

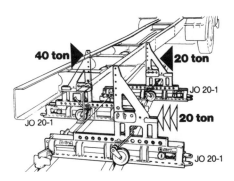

Frame aligning set JO20-40 comb. contains one SR1 trolley with two 20 ton press capacity hydraulic cylinders each. This gives then a total press capacity of 40 tons. In addition to this the set contains two JO20-1 trolleys with one 20 ton press capacity hydraulic cylinder each. The SR1 must always work alone against the two JO20-1 of lesser capacity.

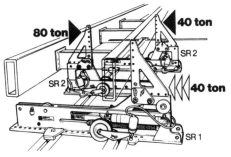

Frame aligning set SK40-BS (the Skanik set, our original system) contains one SR1 of 40 tons press capacity and two non-hydraulic counterstays, the SR2:s. The solo working SR2 withstands 80 tons of pressure developed through leverage when the SR1 trolley presses 40 tons. (see diagram) The SR40-BS is intended for work on very heavy frame members.

EXAMPLES

The following examples are typical for trucks that have been
involved in overturning, collision or damage caused by
erroneously used dumper-tipper or loader equipment.
Suitable alignment equipment is listed for each type of damage
as well as equipment location and use.

Side sways

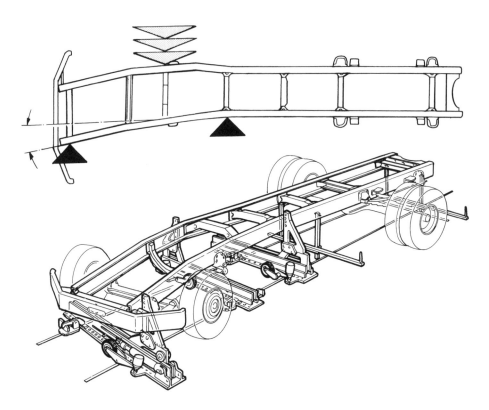

Stiff rear crossmembers are normally at right angles to
the side rails. The front crossmembers are out of
square. If the width of the frame is different in the front
and the rear the damaged area is often found where the
frame starts narrowing to the rear.

The front crossmember is often heavily deformed
because of the large angle alteration which has taken
place in relation to the side rails.

Equipment	Qty
Press trolley SR 1:K or JO 20-1	1
Trolley for anchorage SR 2 or JO 20-1	2
Anchoring arm JO12	6
Press bracket SR6 or SR7	3
Lock pin SR10	6
Lock pin SR12	6
Wedge SR 16-2	6

Vertical bend, front end of one side rail

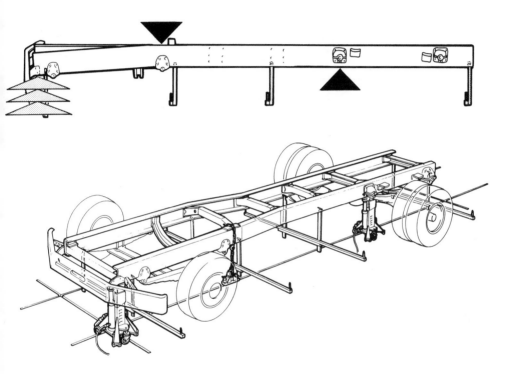

This type of damage can easily be confused with different front spring heights.

The damage is usually found at the rear front spring brackets or by the end of the inner frame. By measuring with a string under the side rails it is possible to establish that one side rail is undamaged. During alignment it then suffices to sight along the frame gauges.

Equipment	Qty
Chain anchorage JO44	1
Chain KL 13-8-3 M	1
Hydraulic jack SR 74MH	2
Protective spacers SR36	

One side rail bent up at rear or other bent down at front

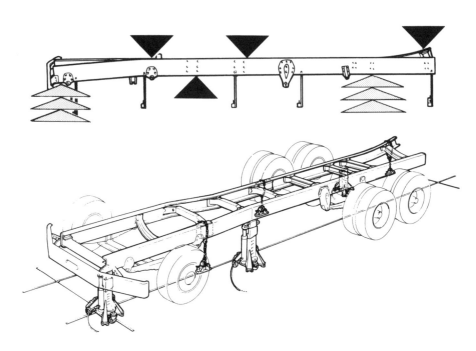

This type of damage is usually found on three-axle trucks.

By sighting from the side it can be established that the frame side rails are in line adjacent to the bogie section but have local damage in front and behind the rear axles.

Equipment	Qty
Chain anchorage JO44	2
Chain KL13-8-3 M	2
Hydraulic jack SR 74 MH	2
Protective spacers SR36	

Vertically bent down, a sag, between front and rear springs

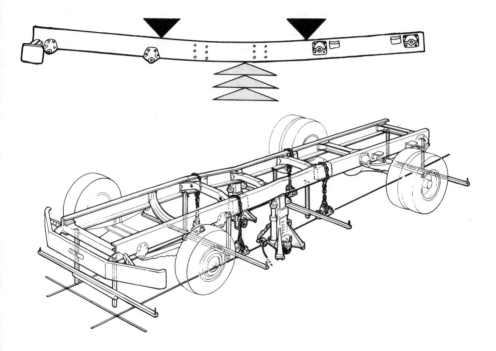

This type of damage is commonly caused by overloading. Often both rails are damaged in a similar way.

Equipment	Qty
Hydraulic jack SR 74 MH	1
Chain anchorage JO 44	2
Chain KL 13-8-3 M	2
Protective spacers SR 36	

Twist

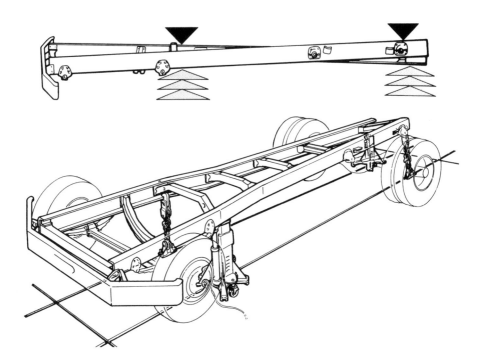

The individual frame rails may be straight but not parallel in relation to each other.
This damage leads to bent crossmember gussets near the ends of the frame.

Equipment	Qty
Hydraulic jack SR 74MH	2
Chain anchorage JO44	2
Hook for U beams SR18-3	2
Chain KL13-8-3 M	2
Protective spacers SR36	

Diamond displacement

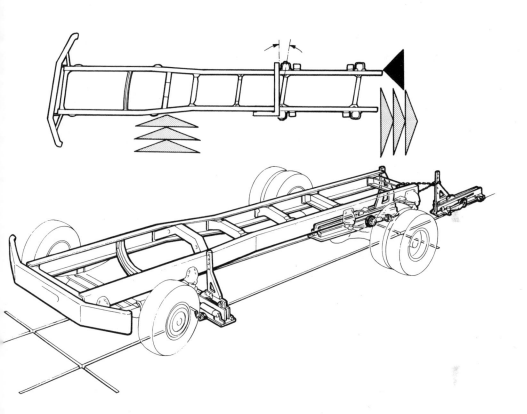

This is most common on two-axle dumper/tipper trucks that have turned over when dumping. This type of damage is unusual on three-axle trucks because of the rigid bogie section.

Equipment	Qty
Set square 20"x40" (500x1000 mm) R-2538-1005	1
Press/pull trolley SR 1:K or JO 20-1	1
Trolley for anchorage SR 2:K	2
Anchoring arm JO12	6
Press bracket SR7 or SR8	3
Lock pin SR10	6
Lock pin SR12	6
Wedge SR16-2	6

If needed, hydraulic cylinder I-CF320 with accessories can be placed diagonally between crossmembers.

Local damage

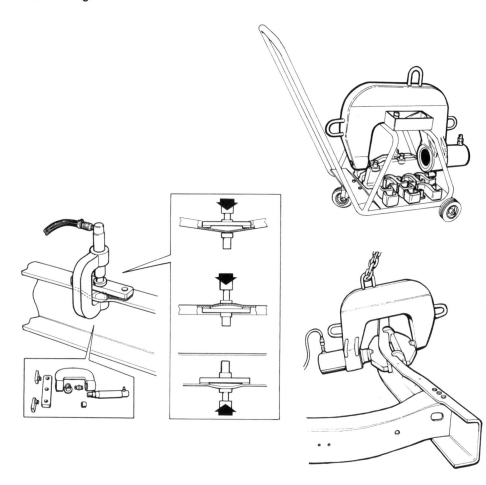

The best tool for straigtening bent flanges is press clamp kit
SR RBS-10.

For local damage where SR RBS-10 with 10-ton press force does not suffice, press clamp SR 450-RB-RSB at 40 tons should be used.

Equipment	Qty
Steel ruler 3 ft (1000 mm) R-2506-0302	1
Press clamp SR31	1
Yoke SR33-1	1
Support plate SR32-2	2
Lock pin SR31-11	1
Cylinder stud I-THR114	1
Hydraulic cylinder I-CF210	1

A4.1.11   *Vehicle alignment is completed within the approved*
          timescales
   Refer to *A2.1.7.*

A4.1.12   *Where the reinstatement is likely to exceed the approved*
          timescale the circumstances are reported promptly to an
          authorised person
   Refer to *A2.1.8.*

A4.1.13   *Reinstatement activities are performed in accordance with*
          statutory and organisational policy and procedure for health
          and safety
   Refer to *A2.1.9.*

A4.2 REMOVE VEHICLE CHASSIS SECTIONS AND PREPARE SURFACES TO RECEIVE NEW SECTIONS

A4.2.1 Appropriate information is accessed from appropriate sources to inform the procedures for the removal of damaged sections
Refer to *A4.1.1* of this (A4LH) section.

A4.2.2 Protective clothing and equipment appropriate to the repair activities are used
Refer to *A4.1.2* of this (A4LH) section.

A4.2.3 Sections not subject to repair are protected, where appropriate, using approved methods and equipment
Refer to *A4.2.3* (Unitary Construction).

A4.2.4 Damage sections are removed using approved methods and equipment
When removing damaged frame sections it may be necessary first to remove parts of the body or cab, or some of the mechanical components; that is, engine, gearbox, suspension or steering or a combination of these.

The method used to remove damaged sections will depend on how they are joined together.

The joining method used with this type of chassis construction could be:

- Welded
- Riveted
- Bolted

The joints of the chassis will be between the crossmembers and the side rails. The side rails, which run the full length of the vehicle, will normally be one piece. The crossmembers, of which there could be up to eight, are attached between the two side rails at specific spacing. At the point of attachment, the joint may be reinforced by the use of a gusset, which may also have to be removed when removing a chassis section.

WELDED JOINTS

Joints which are welded will have to be cut off, initially possibly by burning, followed by final dressing with a grinder to remove all traces of the weld and to allow accurate fitting of the new section. On any areas of

136

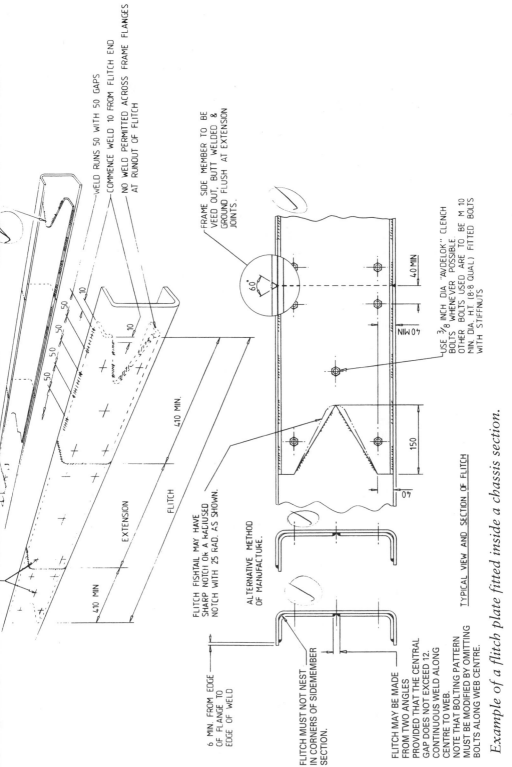

WELD RUNS 50 WITH 50 GAPS

COMMENCE WELD 10 FROM FLITCH END

NO WELD PERMITTED ACROSS FRAME FLANGES AT RUNOUT OF FLITCH

FRAME SIDE MEMBER TO BE VEED OUT, BUTT WELDED & GROUND FLUSH AT EXTENSION JOINTS.

EXTENSION

FLITCH

410 MIN.

410 MIN

FLITCH FISHTAIL MAY HAVE SHARP NOTCH OR A RADIUSED NOTCH WITH 25 RAD. AS SHOWN.

ALTERNATIVE METHOD OF MANUFACTURE.

6 MIN FROM EDGE OF FLANGE TO EDGE OF WELD

FLITCH MUST NOT NEST IN CORNERS OF SIDEMEMBER SECTION.

FLITCH MAY BE MADE FROM TWO ANGLES PROVIDED THAT THE CENTRAL GAP DOES NOT EXCEED 12. CONTINUOUS WELD ALONG CENTRE TO WEB.
NOTE THAT BOLTING PATTERN MUST BE MODIFIED BY OMITTING BOLTS ALONG WEB CENTRE.

60°

40 MIN

40 MIN

150

40

USE 3/8 INCH DIA "AVDELOK" CLENCH BOLTS WHENEVER POSSIBLE OTHER BOLTS USED ARE TO BE M10 MIN. DIA. H.T. (8·8 QUAL) FITTED BOLTS WITH STIFFNUTS

TYPICAL VIEW AND SECTION OF FLITCH

Example of a flitch plate fitted inside a chassis section.

the chassis which may be subjected to excessive stresses, or where a chassis may have been extended, flitch plates will have been inserted within the side rail. If a new flitch is to be fitted, or this area has sustained extensive damage which will necessitate the flitch being removed, it will be removed by grinding out the weld and prising out the flitch. This will help relieve any stresses on the side rail and allow realignment to take place.

BOLTED JOINTS

The majority of chassis frames are constructed using bolted joints. Again it may be necessary to remove areas of the damaged section by burning or sawing to allow access to the bolted area. This will depend on the extent of the damage. The bolts are removed by conventional methods, that is, spanners, ratchet and sockets or pneumatic impact wrenches. If using an impact wrench, always use the special 'Hex' black sockets which are designed to take high impacts. Never use 'multi-point' chrome-vanadium sockets, as they may shatter when subjected to high impacts. The bolts used during a chassis assembly will be made from high-tensile steel with self-locking nuts; they should, therefore, be replaced using the same type of bolts.

With all the bolts removed, the damaged sections can now be removed. It may be necessary to use a hammer to loosen the joints, as they may have become stuck over a period of time or stuck by the application of paint.

RIVETED JOINTS

To remove a member which has been riveted, you will first have to remove the head from one end of the rivet. If the rivets are small, the heads may be chiselled off, but it would be better to grind off the head until the rivet shank is flush with the surface of the chassis member. The rivet can now be removed by using a suitably sized drift and hammer. The drift should be slightly smaller, and longer than, the rivet. This will prevent it becoming jammed as it knocks the rivet out. With all the rivets taken out, the damaged section can now be removed in the same way as the unbolted one.

A4.2.5   Damaged surfaces are restored to a condition suitable for the fitting of new sections

With all the sections removed that are to be replaced, any remaining damage should be rectified prior to fitting the new sections. It may be that one of the sections you have previously removed can be straightened and replaced. Any misalignment remaining will be reinstated using the methods described in *A4.1*.

A4.2.6 *The removal of damaged sections is completed within approved timescales*
Refer to *A2.1.7*.

A4.2.7 *Where the removal of damaged sections is likely to exceed the approved timescales, the circumstances are reported promptly to an authorised person*
Refer to *A2.1.8*.

A4.2.8 *Removal activities are performed in accordance with statutory and organisational policy and procedures for health and safety*
Refer to *A2.1.9*.

A4.3 ALIGN AND FIT REPLACEMENT CHASSIS SECTIONS

A4.3.1 Appropriate information is accessed from appropriate sources to inform the required fitting

Typical information you will require when fitting replacement chassis sections will be related to the methods of joints used. With bolted joints you will have to be aware of the limitations of the various types of bolts and locking nuts, torque settings and spanner and socket sizes.

With riveted joints you will need information on rivet types and the method of forming the rivet heads.

Welded joints will probably be made using Manual Metal Arc (MMA) Welding or Metal Arc Gas Shielded (MAGS) welding or a combination of both. You will need to access information on rod sizes, type of rod to use, type of shielding gas, size of wire gauge and the machine set-up.

A4.3.2 Protective clothing and equipment appropriate to the fitting activities are used

Refer to the final chapter, *A13*, and to *A2.1.2* for general awareness.

A4.3.3 Jig alignment fixtures are prepared and adjusted in accordance with equipment manufacturers' specification

Because most of the replacement sections to be fitted will be supplied pre-drilled, it is likely that no alignment fixtures will be required, provided that the remaining chassis has been reinstated to its correct alignment.

On light vehicles, the procedure laid down in *A4.3.3* (Unitary Construction) should be followed.

A4.3.4 Replacement sections are aligned and secured within the tolerance specified for the particular vehicle

The various tolerances have been outlined in *A4.2*. On average a quarter of an inch (6mm) will be an acceptable tolerance. The new section should be within this allowance to maintain dimensional accuracy of the assembled chassis frame. For bolted sections, all bolts should remain slack until all the new sections are fitted. Using the measurements from the chassis drawing or data sheet, align one section at a time and tighten one or two bolts on each side. This will allow for easy and quick slackening if any minor adjustment is required. It may be necessary to use clamps to aid alignment, especially with welded or riveted sections. At all stages in the fitting process you should check they are aligned correctly.

On light vehicles, the procedures are laid down in *A4.3.4* (Unitary Construction).

A4.3.5 Sections are refitted using approved methods, materials and equipment

The three main methods of fitting the new sections will be:
- Bolted
- Riveted
- Welded

BOLTED JOINTS

With the section fitted and in correct alignment, it will be a simple task of fitting and tightening all the bolts holding the section in place. The main points to adhere to when bolting the chassis member are:
- Always use high-tensile steel bolts of the correct diameter and length.
- Nuts must be either self-locking or used in conjunction with a locking device.
- Tighten nuts and bolts to their specific torque, using a torque wrench.
- Where more than one bolt is used at any joint, tighten each bolt a little at a time.

After all bolts are tightened, re-check the complete assembly for dimensional accuracy and readjust as required.

RIVETED JOINTS

Very few joints will be held together using rivets. If they are, the rivets used should be the same length, diameter and have the same properties as the rivets that were removed.

With riveted joints no adjustment will be capable after the rivet has been set. Because of the large size of the rivets used, a pneumatic rivet set will have to be used.

After the rivets have been set there should be no movement between the joint.

WELDED JOINTS

Two types of welding may be used during the reassembly of the chassis and the selection will depend on the weight of the chassis. On a light-weight chassis, MAGS welding will be the preferred joining method.

Vehicles and trailers which have a heavy chassis frame will usually use Manual Metal Arc (MMA) as the preferred joining method, although MAGS welding could also be used provided the equipment in use is capable of welding that thickness of metal. Whichever method you use, you must be fully experienced and competent to carry out the welding to a very high standard.

When refitting welded sections, they will have been aligned and clamped into position. All sections must be tacked and the clamps taken off as you go along. After all tacking has been carried out, final checking of the alignment should be done before full welding is done.

After welding no adjustments can be made. When welding, all safety precautions must be observed.

The location, type and size of the welds used must mirror that which was used during the manufacturing process.

A4.3.6   Sealents are selected and applied according to the manufacturers' specification for type, method of application and thickness

For general information on sealers, refer to *A4.3.6* (Unitary Construction).

Sealers and primers may be used on the joints before assembly takes place to prevent the ingress of water into the joints. All welds must be cleaned and sealed to prevent the formation of rust in the surfaces.

A4.3.7   The alignment and refitting of sections is completed within approved timescales

Commercial vehicles, buses and trailers differ from private vehicles in that for every hour they are on the road they are making money. Replacement hired vehicles can prove very expensive to an operator while his vehicle is off the road, so it is important that all the work is completed within the time allowed in the estimate.

A4.3.8   Where the alignment and refitting of sections is likely to exceed the approved timescale, the circumstances are reported promptly to an authorised person

Refer to *A2.1.8*.

A4.3.9   Fitting activities are performed in accordance with statutory and organisational policy and procedure for health and safety
Refer to *A2.1.9.*

A6 UNDERPINNING KNOWLEDGE

RE-INSTATE THE CLEANLINESS OF THE VEHICLE

A6.1 CLEAN VEHICLE EXTERIOR

6.1.1 *Appropriate protective clothing and coverings are used during cleaning operations*

Protective clothing is needed to keep you dry and protected from the dirt which is removed from the vehicle while you are carrying out the cleaning tasks.

When hand-washing a vehicle, or finishing the cleaning operation after an automatic car wash, the necessity is to wear waterproof trousers and boots.

When you are using a pressure washer you should wear waterproof trousers, jacket and boots, and safety goggles. You should also protect your hands by wearing heavy-duty rubber gloves.

When you are using a steam cleaner you should ensure that the waterproof trousers, jacket and boots which you wear can withstand an accidental blast of the high temperature, high pressure steam. The material is usually a heavyweight type with a thick rubberised coating. Also, instead of wearing goggles, you need a face mask to protect your entire face from the hot blasts of steam. Your gloves must also be resistant to the occasional blast of steam as well as able to protect you from injury by sharp objects.

When using polish or other cleaning agents you should protect your hands with suitable gloves.

6.1.2 *Cleaning agents are selected in accordance with specifications for vehicle type*

Jet sprays are a very quick and easy way of cleaning cars, but they are also very strong and force water into places where is does not belong. Most new cars can now be cleaned safely with high pressure jet sprays but be careful; using a spray wrongly can cause serious damage to some types of car.

The most common example is 'Cabriolet' cars with a folding fabric roof. Some older cars have fabric sunshine roofs that can cause similar problems. The water seals around the edges of roofs like these can leak very easily under the high pressure of a water jet, and the fabric can also be damaged. The fabric itself can also be damaged by using strong cleaning chemicals. If in doubt use a more gentle way of cleaning, such as a mild detergent and a sponge.

A sponge may be a better way of cleaning areas that cannot be reached by a jet spray, for example inside door shuts.

Be very careful around areas of corroded paintwork and poorly applied coachlines, as these can easily be damaged by a jet spray. Never use a jet spray inside the engine bay of the vehicle without getting permission and advice. Spraying water around an engine can easily damage sophisticated electrical installations and, more importantly, a powerful electric shock could easily damage you!

If in doubt always wash areas by hand. It may be harder work and take more time, but it can save a lot of trouble.

The cleaning agents will usually be the same for all types of dirt and vehicle, but you may need to use special cleaners for grease, oversprayed anti-corrosion treatment, or oversprayed paints. Always be very careful before you use strong cleaning agents. Some are very strong and they can damage plastic parts on the car. If you have any doubts about whether they are suitable for the job, consult your supervisor. Make sure that you wear gloves and goggles if appropriate.

6.1.3 Cleaning agents are used according to cleaning agent manufacturers' instructions

You should also refer to 6.1.2 above. As well as ensuring that the cleaning agent is used for the correct application, you must also ensure that you use it in the correct way. Often cleaning agents are used diluted with water and the correct proportions of chemical (agent) to water must be used. Use a graduated measuring jug; do not guess volumes. Temperature is an important factor as it brings about chemical changes to the cleaning agent, so ensure that the correct temperature is used and maintained. Acid, alkali and solvent-based cleaners need time to act against the dirt, but if they are left on too long the chemical may cause damage to the part it is supposed to be cleaning.

Before using any cleaning agent you should read the instructions.

Because of the nature of cleaning agents, they are mostly poisonous and will irritate the skin and cause severe damage to your eyes. Therefore do not swallow and keep away from skin and eyes.

6.1.4 *External surfaces of vehicle are cleaned in accordance with customer contract and to schedule*

The condition of a vehicle after the repairs is very important to the customer. If the vehicle is very clean when it is handed back to the customer, it gives a good impression about the way your company cares for its customers' cars. Even though the repairs may have been very small, the customer will appreciate your effort in cleaning the car. The repairs will look even better if the whole car is looking clean and shiny. This is why most insurance companies will expect the customer's car to be cleaned thoroughly after the repairs, and it is often an important part of the work that your company has agreed to do (some garages choose to clean the car before the repairs are even started; this helps to keep the workshops clean, as well as making the repairs easier).

Your company will be able to tell you how thoroughly they expect the cleaning to be done, but you should pay particular attention to dirt and dust that has collected on the car during the repairs. Look out especially for greasy finger marks! Start from the top of the vehicle and work your way down methodically to make sure that you do not miss any areas. Remember to clean the wheels and tyres, inside door, bonnet and boot/tailgate checks.

Remember that the customers are having to make do without their car while the repairs are carried out. Even if the customer has been supplied with a courtesy car, your company will want to have the courtesy car back as soon as possible, so it is important that the repairs do not take too long. Cleaning the car will be the very last part of the repairs so it must be completed on time.

If you will not have enough time to finish the cleaning properly make sure that you tell your supervisor.

6.1.5 *The cleaned vehicle is free from any residual cleaning agents*

Once you have finished cleaning off the exterior dirt the vehicle should be rinsed off thoroughly with clean water . If any cleaning agent is left on the car it will leave an ugly mark when it dries, so the final rinse is very important. If possible you should always use a leather to dry the vehicle after you have rinsed it; this will make sure that the water does not leave any marks as it dries.

6.1.6 Used cleaning agents and waste materials are safely disposed of according to statutory and organisational requirements

Just like any other chemicals used in the workplace, cleaning agents can contain strong chemicals that need to be handled and disposed of carefully. Your company may need to keep records of how it disposes of these chemicals and there are laws covering this. Many chemicals have to be collected and disposed of by licensed carriers.

The soaps that are used to wash the exterior will be safe when diluted correctly in accordance with the manufacturers' instructions. Never pour other chemicals down a drain without the approval of a supervisor. Many chemicals are controlled under the Environmental Protection Act (EPA) which will stipulate how they are disposed of.

6.1.7 Damage to vehicle or trims is noted and reported promptly to the appropriate person

Before you start cleaning a vehicle you should visually inspect it for accident damage and other faults. Any damage found should then be reported to your supervisor immediately. Many companies use a pro-forma for recording damage. This is a form with a diagram which shows views of all the sides of the vehicle. You mark the diagram with an arrow to indicate the damaged area and write a brief comment at the side - for example, 'dent at bottom of door'. If the vehicle is very dirty, especially when caked in mud as many off-road and goods vehicles are, damage may not be visible until the damaged area is cleaned. In this case your supervisor must be told immediately and the appropriate damage pro-forma completed.

6.1.8 Cleaning activities are performed in accordance with statutory and organisational policy and procedure for health and safety

As was listed in 6.1.1, the correct PPE must be worn when carrying out cleaning activities.

When not carrying out wet operations, normal overalls should be worn, that is cotton boiler suit and safety shoes/boots. Protective gloves should be worn when using or handling cleaning agents and goggles must be worn where there is a risk of harmful substances entering your eyes.

Where there is the use of water this must be done in a wash bay with an approved drainage system. Solvent-based chemicals must not be allowed to enter the drains.

A6.2 CLEAN THE INTERIOR OF THE VEHICLE/SOFT TRIM SURFACES

6.2.1. Appropriate protective clothing and coverings are used during cleaning operations.

Whenever you are working on a vehicle, the appropriate overalls, safety footwear and PPE must be worn. When working inside a vehicle your overalls must be free from oil and grease. Seat covers and paper floor mats should be used when driving the vehicle. If the steering wheel is of the soft-touch leather/suede type, then this should be covered with a plastic sleeve.

If you are using cleaning agents, rubber protective gloves must be used.

If you are using cleaning equipment where dust is generated, or cleaning agents are under pressure, then goggles must be worn.

6.2.2. Items extraneous to the vehicle interior are removed before and replaced after cleaning

The first thing to do is remove anything from the car that could get in the way of your cleaning (or be sucked up in the vacuum cleaner by mistake!) - this means the personal items that the customer has put on the dashboard, in the door pockets, or anywhere else (except areas with lids on, such as the glove compartment or cassette box). As you remove these items BE VERY CAREFUL. Make a note of where you found them, so that they can be put back in the right place. NEVER throw anything away: you do not know if the owner wants to keep it or not! Put everything you remove in a safe place while you clean the vehicle.

The other items to remove are the floor mats, which will be easier to clean outside the vehicle. Having them out of the way will help you clean the interior carpets too.

Do not remove any seat covers (except the plastic ones that have been put in the vehicle during the repairs). Never touch the controls on the car radio or put the radio on while you are cleaning the car. You risk running down the battery, and nothing upsets a customer more than finding the settings have been changed on the radio!

After you have cleaned the interior, carefully replace all the items you have removed. Make sure they are put back where you found them.

6.2.3 Cleaning and finishing agents are used according to manufacturers' instructions

As with all chemical cleaning agents, you must always read the instructions before you use them. You must then follow the instructions closely.

Many agents are mixed with water before use. Ensure that you use the correct proportions; use a graduated measuring jug for this.

The pure wool carpets in quality cars may shrink if they are wet. Check the carpet material against the cleaning agent. This can also apply to the roof lining and other upholstery.

Solvent-based cleaning agents will dissolve certain types of plastic materials. Be careful where you use these or the seats might start to disappear before your eyes.

Dashboards are made from a variety of materials and are not always what they appear. Many dashboards which appear to be wood are, in fact, plastic, so be careful with the choice of chemical cleaning agents. One story is of an apprentice who was cleaning the inside of a Rolls Royce when he noticed a mark on the 'wooden' dashboard which had been made during the repair. This was a very small line mark, but this young chap was not going to report the fact to the foreman. He said that he had repaired marks like this in CDT/woodwork lessons at school and off he went to get some very fine abrasive paper. Fifteen minutes later it seemed that the foreman was going to kill him. The area of the dashboard was now a bright metal colour; the 'wood effect' on this model was, in fact, a photographic image.

6.2.4 Interior surfaces of the vehicle are cleaned in accordance with customer contract and to schedule

You will have made a contract with the customer to carry out the cleaning in a particular manner or to cover certain parts of the interior. These should be carried out within the agreed time scale.

The tasks may include the following:
- vacuuming the carpets and seats
- cleaning the headlining
- shampooing the carpets and seats
- cleaning the dashboard/facia area
- cleaning/shampooing the other interior trim (door panels etc).
- cleaning/polishing other interior surfaces

6.2.5 Appropriate cleaning and finishing agents are applied to appropriate surfaces

There are many different types of surface inside a car, and each type of surface can require a different cleaner to be used. A cleaning agent suitable for plastic dashboards could badly damage a leather seat cover.

The main types of surface are:
Glass
Hard plastic (dashboards etc.)
Leather-effect plastic (door linings, gearstick gaiters etc)
Leather (seats)
Fabric (seats)
Carpet
Flock (roof linings)

It is possible to have a different type of cleaner for each surface.

6.2.6 The cleaned interior is free from residual cleaning and finishing agents

No matter how thoroughly you clean the car, the work will be wasted if you do not clean off the cleaning agents completely (this is a particular problem on the interior surfaces of windscreens, where residual marks can only be seen at night or in low, strong sunlight).

The main trick to remember is always to use a clean cloth. A dirty cloth will leave a trail of marks while you are cleaning and make your job much harder. Have a dispenser of clean wipes handy while you are working. Work methodically, cleaning one area at a time.

Remember, a smeared windscreen can impair the vision of the driver at night when faced with on-coming traffic.

6.2.7. Used cleaning agents and waste materials are safely disposed of according to statutory and organisational requirements

Once a container of cleaning agent is empty it should immediately be disposed of properly. This does not necessarily mean putting it in a waste skip. Any waste with traces of the chemicals used in painting and cleaning cars may need to be disposed of safely by a registered specialist.

Used cloths and disposable wipes should be put in a bin with a lid on as soon as they are finished with, then disposed of in a sealed plastic sack. Again, do not necessarily put them in a normal skip; they may be disposed of with the other special waste. It is a legal obligation to dispose of chemicals and solvents as indicated by the Environmental Protection Act (EPA).

6.2.8. *Faults or damage to the vehicle interior are promptly reported to appropriate persons*

Remember that the interior of the vehicle might have been damaged while it was under repair. This may be small tears in the seat fabric, burn marks from stray sparks, MAGS welding spatter on exterior glass, or heavy soiling from grease that you are unable to clean. Obviously, it is very important for any damage to be reported as soon as possible.

The damage may have been caused before the vehicle came in for repair. In this case the customer may know about it, or it may have been noted by the workshop supervisor when the vehicle came in for repair. If the damage was done during the repairs it must be put right, if possible before the vehicle is handed back to the customer.

As you clean the car you should be constantly aware of this responsibility.

6.2.9 *Cleaning activities are performed in accordance with statutory and organisational policy and procedure for health and safety*

When carrying out interior cleaning operations you must wear the appropriate PPE and the recommended overalls and safety footwear. In terms of PPE, this means protective gloves when using cleaning agents, and goggles when dust or other material may be splashed into your eyes.

Wet cleaning operations must be carried out in the appropriate washbay area where there is an approved drainage system.

The cleaning agents used must be those approved by your company.

A special point for consideration is that most cleaning/finishing agents give off some form of fumes. These can affect different people in different ways. Do NOT use any cleaning agents inside a vehicle with the doors closed. Always try to work in a well-ventilated area, and ensure that somebody knows where you are working.

Use a dust-mask over your nose and mouth if cleaning generates dust. A vacuum cleaner with a long flexible hose and a remote cylinder will reduce the risk of exposure to dust.

UNIT A9L.2 UNDERPINNING KNOWLEDGE

REMOVE AND REPLACE VEHICLE COMPONENTS/UNITS

A9.1 DISMANTLE VEHICLE SYSTEMS TO REMOVE COMPONENTS/SYSTEMS

A9.1.1 Appropriate protective clothing and coverings are used during the dismantling activities
Refer to *A2.1.2*.

A9.1.2 Appropriate information is accessed from appropriate sources to inform the dismantling of systems
Refer to *A2.1.1*.

A9.1.3 Equipment used in dismantling is confirmed safe prior to use and operated in the approved safe manner
Before you use any tools or equipment you should always check that they are safe to use. You should also check that they will do their job properly.

Nine points which will add to the life of the tool and the vehicle are:
1. Confirm that the Safe Working Load (SWL) of all lifting equipment is sufficient for the job, including any ropes or slings.
2. Check electrical equipment for the condition of the wire and plug.
3. Check air tools for condition, especially leaks; apply lubricant if it is needed.
4. Ensure that any special tools which screw on to the vehicle or component are the correct thread and that the thread is not damaged.
5. Check that mandrills or protective pads are fitted where they are needed.
6. Avoid the use of unnecessary force.
7. Do not hammer tools which are not designed for hammering.
8. Do not lever or pry against soft surfaces or brittle materials.
9. Keep tools clean and replace in the store after use.

The final chapter, *A13* gives more information on health and safety matters.

A9.1.4   Dismantling is carried out in accordance with manufacturers'
recommendations/procedures in respect to isolation and
removal of components and units

Before starting any dismantling, you should read the appropriate part of the workshop manual and ensure that you understand exactly what you are doing. You must ensure that you have any special tools which are needed for the task and if assistance is required check that it is available. In other words, you need to plan your job so that you can carry it out in the correct manner.

Some points which need special attention are:

*   Before working on the electrical system always disconnect the battery, but before you disconnect the battery ensure that you remove the code from the stereo and confirm any setting on any other ROMs which might have volatile memories, for example the ignition/fuel ECU or ABS. If you are going to remove only one component, it may be easier just to remove the fuse or relay from the circuit concerned. For instance, if you are just going to remove the radiator then you only need to remove the fuse or relay from the electric cooling fan circuit to prevent the fan from accidentally operating while your fingers are in that area.

*   Isolate the diesel fuel pump from the supply line and plug the end of the supply line before you start to disconnect any other of the fuel lines from the pump. This reduces the risk of accidental fuel flow from the tank.

*   If possible use pipe clamps on the brake hoses to isolate the wheel cylinders or callipers from the system before removing these parts. This prevents the spillage and loss of excess brake fluid and reduces the need to 'bleed' the rest of the brake system.

A9.1.5   Dismantling minimises risk of damage to other vehicle
systems

If you have carried out the requirements for *A9.1.3* and *A9.1.4* you will have done a lot of work towards this PC too. You should also read this in conjunction with the next PC, *A9.1.6*.

If you have properly read the manual you will know which part comes off the vehicle in which order. If you remove the parts in this logical order you will not have any problems and you will not damage any other parts or systems. Do not try to take short cuts or miss out steps. The old saying 'more haste less speed' was written specially for impatient vehicle technicians.

A9.1.6   Correct specialist tools/equipment are used where required for dismantling

All good workshops have a range of special tools; main dealers automatically buy the special tools for each new model as it is introduced. If you do not have the special tool for the job in hand you have a number of options:
- buy one
- hire one
- make one
- sub-contract the job to somebody who has the tool

Each of these options will cost an amount of cash, but the cost will be less than the damage that you are likely to cause by trying to 'bodge'. Increasing your special tool collection has two advantages, you will do the job faster and so make more profit and you'll have the tool for the next time that you do the job. As a mechanic/technician you will be wanting to increase your collection of special tools. How many of these items have you got in your tool kit?

sump plug tool
gearbox/transmission filler plug tool
long-reach spark plug socket
wire strippers/crimping tool
flywheel puller
hub puller
brake bleeding tool
pick-up magnet
ball-joint splitter
spring compressors
brake-pipe clamp
cir-clip pliers

Which of these tools are there in the workshop where you work?

tyre removing machine
hub puller
air conditioning equipment evacuating/re-filling machine
hydro/pneumatic suspension discharger/pump
engine hoist
gearbox jack
overhead gantry
flywheel puller
petrol tank drainer
brake dust vacuum

continue on page 160

Removing rear-hub using a 2-leg puller.

Drawing half-shaft out of axle casing using a sliding-hammer.

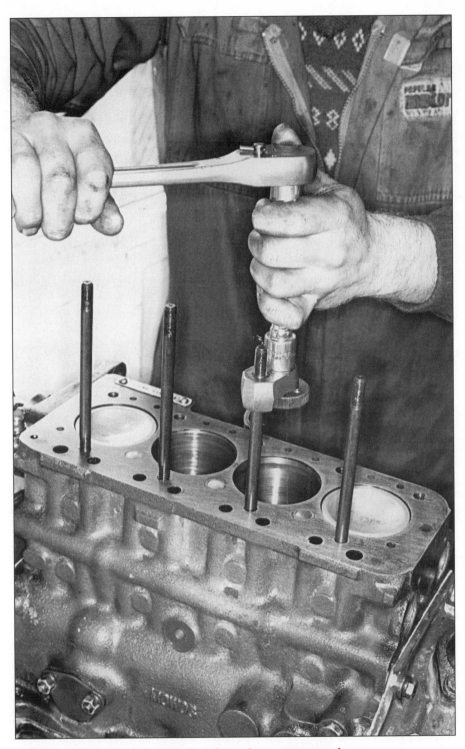

Removing cylinder head stud with stud removing tool.

Measuring oil pump clerarance with feeler gauges.

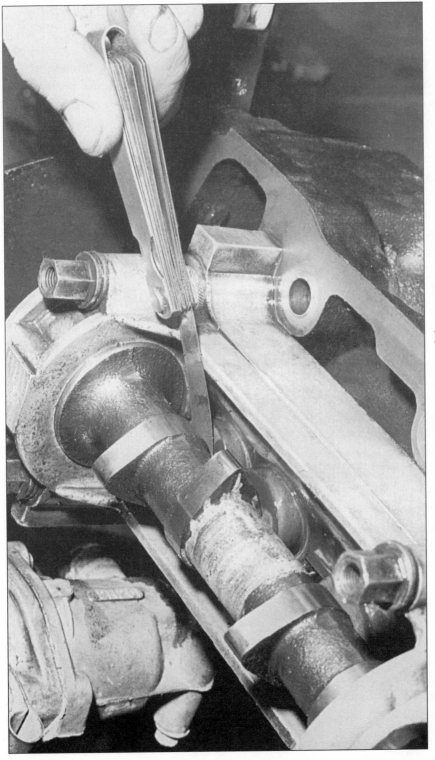

Measuring valve clearance with feeler gauges, note the position of the cam.

A9.1.7 Additional faults or potential faults noticed are reported to appropriate authority promptly

When you are dismantling a system or removing a component, you should keep your eyes open for any other faulty or damaged parts. If you spot a fault, or an item which has a potential fault, you must report this to your supervisor. For instance, if you are removing the gearbox and note that an adjacent engine mounting is cracked and will soon break, this should be noted on the job card and pointed out to your supervisor when the gearbox is removed. This will prevent the vehicle from breaking down unnecessarily, so saving the customer money and possibly preventing complaints about the original repair. Customers frequently, wrongly, blame the garage for any breakdowns which happen after service or repair jobs. If you report potential faults you reduce the risk of complaints and add to customer satisfaction.

A9.1.8 Risk of contact with/leakage of /contamination by hazardous substances is minimised

Before you start to remove any component you should ask yourself: will any liquid or gas escape? If the answer is yes, then you must work out how you are going to prevent it escaping or minimise the loss. If some loss is likely you must also provide a means of catching it and preventing the liquid/gas from staining or defacing any other components.

Let's have a look at some of the common problems:

Cooling systems contain **anti-freeze** which may damage paintwork and you do not want large pools of coolant on the garage floor. Very few cooling systems have drain taps or plugs (all the old vehicles before about 1960 did!). So to minimise the risk of spilling coolant, obtain a drain tray which is deep enough to hold all the contents of the system - usually about 10 litres, but see the data book. Then remove the hose from the lowest point of the system - the bottom hose - having placed the drain tray so that it will collect the coolant as it leaves this joint. Beware of the coolant flowing on to a chassis member and flowing away from the drain tray. You could use a section of roof guttering to direct the coolant into the drain tray.

If you are going to remove a wheel cylinder or brake calliper then some **brake fluid** is going to escape. Brake fluid is like paint stripper if it comes into contact with the vehicle bodywork. Use a hose clamp on the nearest flexible hose and place a drip tray underneath the brake assembly which you are working on.

Before you remove an engine, drain all the **lubricating oil.** It is best to do this when the engine is warm as the oil drains out faster. The same applies to transmission components such as gearboxes and axles.

Petrol is a special hazard. Before you remove a petrol tank it must be pumped dry, using a special petrol-draining pump and enclosed tank. Make sure that the petrol-drainer is connected to the vehicle with an earth cable to prevent the risk of explosion through the discharge of the static electricity which is generated by the flow of petrol.

Diesel fuel is not as explosive as petrol, but the tank should be drained in the same way. Spillage of diesel fuel on the garage floor is a hazard as it does not dry up naturally, it can foul the soles of your shoes and be transferred to the vehicle's interior, where it will stain and cause a bad smell.

A9.1.9 Where appropriate to do so, system features and characteristics are recorded clearly and accurately during dismantling

Dismantling vehicles is easy, putting them back together is difficult, especially if you cannot remember the order of assembly or which position which part fits in. Okay, so you can remember where all the screws go, but which screw came from which hole? On motor cycles this can be a real problem, as often a screw may do two jobs and therefore you'll find ones of different lengths and different thread forms in the same housing.

It is good practice to put all the parts into a parts tray. For components like crankcase screws on motor cycles, cylinder-head bolts and push rods, use some form of device to keep the parts separate and in order. A piece of card with holes punched in is sufficient, write top or front on the card so that you know which way round it should be.

For complicated items, especially wiring connections, it is a good idea to use a notebook. Make a sketch and label the parts or wire colours.

A9.1.10 The dismantling is completed within approved time scales

The manufacturer's time schedule or standard times manual will set the time allowed for the task to be completed. You should be able to complete the task within this time limit.

A9.1.11   *Where the dismantling is likely to exceed the approved timescale, the circumstances are reported promptly to an authorised person*

Refer to *A2.1.8*.

A9.1.12   *Dismantling activities are performed in accordance with statutory and organisational policy and procedure for health and safety*

Refer to the final chapter *A13* for full health and safety information.

A9.2   INSPECT AND TEST SUSPECTED FAULTY COMPONENTS/UNITS

A9.2.1   Appropriate protective clothing and coverings are used during inspection and testing activities

Refer to *A2.1.2.*

A9.2.2   Appropriate information is accessed from appropriate sources to inform the inspection and testing of components/units

Refer to *A2.1.1.*

A9.2.3   Tests on components/units are performed using approved methods and equipment

Before attempting to test any component/unit, you should read the relevant part of the workshop manual, so that you know that you are doing the job in the correct and safe way. Misuse of test equipment can damage the component which is being tested.

The equipment which you use at level 2 are hand-held test instruments, electrical meters and measuring instruments.

You should be able to:
* use a steel rule and calliper to read to an accuracy of 0.5 mm (or 1/32 inch)
* read external and internal micrometers to 0.01 mm (or 0.001 inch)
* use a multimeter to take amp/volt/ohm reading

A9.2.4   Condition and performance of components/units are compared with required operating specifications

With the components/units now removed from the vehicle you may be able to carry out more detailed tests and compare the data with that of the published vehicle specifications. You are advised to set this data out in the form of a table. This is especially important where there is a tolerance band and you need to see how far a component is outside the manufacturers' tolerance.

A9.2.5   Components/units confirmed as faulty are identified for repair or replacement to achieve the most cost-effective outcome

The term 'cost-effective outcome' can be viewed on a long-term basis or as a short-term cure. You need to add together the cost of both the parts and the labour to calculate the cost. If there is a number of options, the advantages and disadvantages of each option must be explained to the customer.

Let us look at an example. An engine has worn or damaged piston rings, but otherwise is in fair-to-good condition. Fitting new piston rings will be a low cost for parts but involve a lot of labour; an exchange engine would be much more expensive on parts but cheap for labour. The piston ring repair might last 20,000 miles; the new engine should be good for 100,000 miles. When you have explained this to the customer let him make up his own mind.

A9.2.6 Advice is sought where fault cannot be attributed to component/unit

If, when you have removed a part from a vehicle, it is not clear whether or not that is the cause of the problem, you should seek advice from your supervisor.

A9.2.7 Documentation relating to the completed inspection and testing of components/units is complete and accurate and passed on to the appropriate authorised person promptly

This PC follows on from A9.2.4. It means that, when you have completed the inspection or testing of the components and recorded your results, you must pass this information on to your supervisor. Passing this information on promptly prevents any time being lost unnecessarily should spare parts or replacement components have to be ordered. This is even more important should you be working a vehicle that is not a common make or one where spares have to be ordered from abroad.

A9.2.8 The inspection and testing is completed within approved timescales

Refer to A9.1.10.

A9.2.9 Where the inspection and testing is likely to exceed the approved timescale. the circumstances are reported promptly to an authorised person

Refer to A2.1.8.

A9.2.10 Inspection and testing activities are performed in accordance with statutory and organisational policy and procedure for health and safety

Refer to the final chapter, Unit A13, for health and safety matters.

A9.3 REPLACE COMPONENTS/UNITS AND REASSEMBLE VEHICLE SYSTEMS

A9.3.1 Appropriate information is accessed from the appropriate source to inform the reassembly of vehicle systems
Refer to *A2.1.1*.

A9.3.2 Appropriate protective clothing and coverings are used during reassembly
Refer to *A2.1.2*.

A9.3.3 Replacement components/units conform to vehicle specification
You should, where possible, always use genuine manufacturers' replacement parts. Some parts carry 'E' numbers to show that they comply with EU regulations; others have type-approval numbers. Type-approval numbers are very important on HGVs/PSVs - fitting non-standard parts may make the use of such a vehicle illegal. As the mechanic/technician fitting the parts, you are responsible in law to ensure that the vehicle complies with the various regulations.

In addition to the legal requirements, you should ensure that the replacement parts match the specification of the originals. Top-of-the-range models may have components/units with enhanced functions which are not obvious until they are checked out.

Items or components/units not specified as OE (Original Equipment) parts may function perfectly adequately but their life span may be shorter and their guarantee may not be as comprehensive as that of OE parts. In addition, the fitting of such components/units may render the vehicle warranty void.

Items that MAY fall into this category include tyres, batteries, brake pads and shoes and timing belts.

A9.3.4 Equipment used in reassembly is confirmed safe prior to use and is operated in the approved safe manner
Refer to *A9.1.3*.

continues on page 170

Removing hub and disc assembly from drive shaft.

Using soft mallet to separate CV joint from drive shaft.

External cir-clip which locates CV joint, check that this is in good condition before re-assembly.

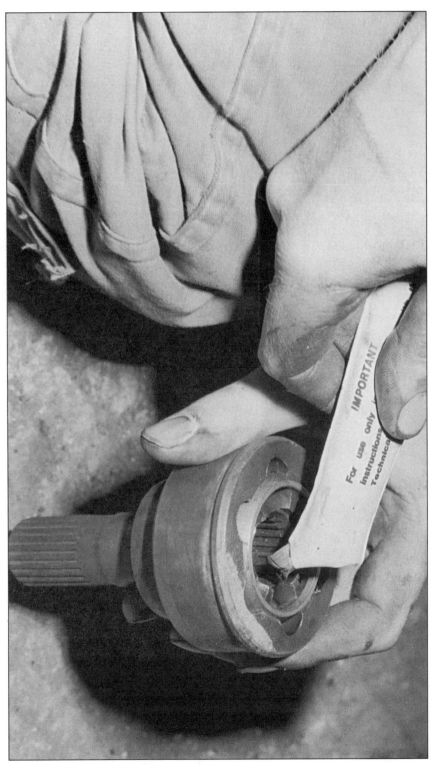

Always use the correct grease, in this CV joint a 'moly' grease is being used.

A9.3.5   Reassembly is carried out in accordance with manufacturers'
recommendations/procedures in respect of the fitting of
components/units

This PC follows on from A9.1.4. Reassembly usually follows dismantling in the workshop manual. This section should be studied before starting work.

It should be borne in mind that, if high-tensile bolts are specified by a manufacturer, then these must be used. You do not want the vehicle failing, do you? See also *A9.3.3*. The choice of parts also applies to the choice of the fixings and fittings.

The main difference between dismantling and reassembly is that many items must be tightened to a specific torque. Nuts and bolts that have not been tightened to a high enough torque may slacken with the vibration of the engine or the running of the vehicle, whereas over-tightening of bolts and nuts may result in them fracturing when they come under stress. Information on specific torque settings can found in the vehicle workshop manual.

A9.3.6   Components/units are adjusted to ensure specified system
operation after fitting

You should adjust each component or unit as your refit it, then you will ensure that it operates correctly when the assembly is complete. This is especially important for items which are covered up when the reassembly is complete.

Information on service adjustments and system replenishment is available from the workshop manual or Autodata books.

Some systems and components may require further adjustment or replacement after a running or settling-in period. This should be noted and carried out accordingly.

A9.3.7   Reassembly minimises risk of damage to the vehicle and its
systems

If you follow the manufacturers' instructions on reassembly procedures, you will have little risk of causing any damage to the vehicle. Sometimes you may be tempted to take short cuts or get flustered during the task. If you plan the task and take each part a step at a time you will have no problems. You should also refer to *A9.3.5*.

*A9.3.8   Documentation relating to the completed rectification is
           complete and accurate and passed to the appropriate person
           promptly*
Refer to *A9.2.7.*

A9.3.9   Reassembly is completed within approved timescales
Refer to *A9.1.10.*

*A9.3.10 Where reassembly is likely to exceed the approved timescales,
an appropriate authorised person is informed promptly*
Refer to *A2.1.8* and *A2.2.9.*

*A9.3.11   Reassembly is performed in accordance with statutory and
            organisational policy and procedure for health and safety*
Refer to *A1.3.9* for health and safety matters.

A9.4 EVALUATE PERFORMANCE OF REASSEMBLED SYSTEMS

A9.4.1 Appropriate information is accessed from appropriate source to inform the evaluation of repaired systems

Refer to *A2.1.1.*

A9.4.2 Evaluation carried out is appropriate to type of repair and is conducted using approved methods and equipment

Evaluation of the rectification is usually carried out by using diagnostic and alignment equipment. This may be the same equipment that was used to trace the faults before the work was carried out.

A9.4.3 Information collected is compared with vehicle specification to confirm rectification of system faults

In PC 9.2.4 you compared the performance of the components with that of the required operating specifications. If your results of the tasks were recorded in the form of a table, you could also compare the new readings with the original (faulty) reading and see the difference which your work has made.

The readings taken after the rectification work should now be within the manufacturers' specifications.

A9.4.4 Where evaluation indicates further variances in system performance, appropriate authority is informed and appropriate remedial action is taken promptly

If the rectification work has not cured the fault, you must immediately inform your supervisor so that he can make a decision as to the next step to be taken.

A9.4.5 Where applicable, repaired systems comply with appropriate statutory requirements

If regulations apply to the system, such as exhaust emissions, the repaired system must comply with these regulations. You, as the mechanic/technician, are legally responsible to ensure that the appropriate regulations are complied with before the vehicle is handed back to the customer. If they do not comply for a reason beyond your control, you must record this on the job card and inform your supervisor.

A9.4.6   Records relating to the evaluation are complete, accurate and
in the correct format

When you carry out diagnostic work you must record your findings, either for your own use as you rectify the fault or for another person who may be involved in the repair process later. This information may also be required for your own company records or for the customer's service records. The information needs to be recorded accurately and in a way in which it can be easily understood. Two ways of doing this are to write it on the job card or on a special form for the purpose. Specialist diagnostic equipment may be supplied with some type of proforma for writing the results in against specific headings, but the move is now towards equipment which has a built-in printer so that the results are printed out at the touch of a button. This is especially useful if you do a print-out before any work is done and compare it to the results when the rectification is complete.

A9.4.7   Evaluation is completed within the approved timescale
Refer to *A9.1.10*.

A9.4.8   Where evaluation is likely to exceed the approved timescale,
an appropriate authorised person is informed promptly
Refer to *A2.1.8* and *A2.2.9*.

A9.4.9   Evaluation activities are performed in accordance with
statutory and organisational policy for health and safety
Refer to *A2.1.9* and to the last chapter, *Unit A13*, for health and safety information.

A10 UNDERPINNING KNOWLEDGE

AUGMENT VEHICLE BODYWORK TO MEET CUSTOMERS' REQUIREMENTS

A10.1 ADVISE CUSTOMERS ON THE AUGMENTATION OF VEHICLE BODYWORK

A10.1.1 Appropriate information is accessed from the appropriate source to inform customers on the augmentation of vehicle bodywork

A great many vehicles now have some enhanced features on the bodywork that the owner has chosen to add. Augmented bodywork can make a car appear more distinctive and allow the owner to make the car stand out from the rest. Bodywork can also be enhanced to help improve the vehicle's performance (or at least give that impression).

There are a very large number of modifications or additions that can be made, and customers will need specialist advice before making any changes to the vehicle to help them choose what work they want doing. You must make sure that you take the trouble to advise them properly before any work is started, and this in turn means making sure you have all the information you need.

Bodywork augmentation is now big business and there is no shortage of information available if you want it. Sources of information fall into three categories:
1. Vehicle manufacturers
2. Specialist parts manufacturers and distributors
3. Paint manufacturers and distributors

Specialist parts, such as spoilers and sill extensions, are manufactured by specialists who will supply very good brochures to demonstrate the applications of their products. Your company may choose to specialise in one type of vehicle and build up expertise about the augmentation available for that type. Otherwise, you will need to spend some time getting the information you need.

Specialist paint finishes can be shown from the manufacturers' colour book, although it is very difficult to give a good impression of what the whole car will look like when it is painted. This is especially true of specialist paint finishes such as 'pearl' effects.

10.1.2 The features and benefits of components which augment vehicle bodywork are described clearly and accurately to the customer

Your customers will be spending a lot of money on improving the vehicle and they deserve a lot of help and guidance in deciding what work is to be done. Remember always that it is their car, not yours, which is having the money spent on it, so try not to let your own personal ideas and tastes affect the way you advise the customer. At the same time, you will probably have more knowledge and experience than the customer, so he could be relying on you for ideas and advice.

This is where the information that you have acquired will be a great advantage, because you will be able to show the customer the range of work that can be done to the vehicle and perhaps suggest ideas that the customer had not thought of.

Colour coding. This can greatly enhances the appearance of a vehicle for relatively low cost. Even if a vehicle is having accident repairs, the owner may consider having items such as door handles, body mouldings, and wing mirror housings painted the same colour as the bodywork at the same time. For relatively little cost the appearance of the vehicle can be enhanced enormously.

Additional panels. Front and rear spoilers are a well-accepted way of setting a car apart and they can improve the looks of a vehicle beyond all recognition. Sill extensions can complete the package. These parts can improve the stability of the car at high speed. It is worth pointing out, too, that a car with individual looks will be less attractive to thieves since it is more distinctive.

Modified panels. Some owners will fit vents to the bonnet to improve engine-bay cooling. In some extreme cases, modified front and rear wings will need to be fitted to allow for modified suspension that will give better grip or a lower ride height.

Specialist finishes. Bodywork repairers are used to dealing with a wide range of paint finishes, and these can be used to improve a vehicle's appearance while at the same time replacing existing damaged paintwork.

Emphasise the benefits of having parts fitted and painted professionally. A poorly-fitted part will make the vehicle appear worse than before and may compromise safety. Your company will be able to offer a warranty on the work it does and give the customer professional reassurance.

Always remember that the customer is not used to dealing with cars every day and will not be at home using technical terms. When you are talking about the work that can be done, take the time to explain what you mean. The customer does not want to be baffled by motor-trade language and it is important that he feels comfortable with what you are suggesting. It is also worth remembering that, if you explain the work fully, the customer will understand how much work is involved and so be more prepared to pay a fair price.

A10.1.3   Where appropriate to do so, any disadvantages associated with the fitting of components which augment vehicle bodywork are described clearly and accurately to the customer

The customer may be spending a lot of money on the improvements to the vehicle, so it is important that he is informed about any potential problems with fitting any extra parts to the vehicle.

These will fall into three main areas:

Problems associated with the attachment of components. Items such as spoilers and skirts will be usually either riveted or bonded to the vehicle. Although you will be as professional as possible when fitting the components, it may be necessary to leave some rivet heads exposed, for example inside door apertures in the case of side skirts. This can be unsightly and some customers may take exception and want to discuss other methods of attachment. The customer should be fully aware of the planned method of attachment before work is started.

Limitations to use of the vehicle arising from the attachment of components. When you are fitting any components the customers should be reminded of how their use of the vehicle could be affected. A low front spoiler will mean problems with curbs and rough ground. Rear vision out of the vehicle may be impaired by additional spoilers and additional trims may not take kindly to rough treatment in automatic car washes.

Problems associated with later removal of components. If the customer should ever want the additional components removed there could be a lot of work involved. Rivet holes will need welding up and repainting. Once parts have been bonded to the car they are very difficult to remove without damaging paintwork or thin metal like you find used in rear quarter panels. If the parts are ever removed it is likely to involve extensive repairs and paintwork. For these reasons, fitting additional components should be regarded as a once-and-for-ever exercise and this should be fully explained to the customer before any work is started.

A10.1.4 Where appropriate, the customer is advised of any
implication for warranty provisions arising from
augmentation of vehicle bodywork

It is unusual for a manufacturer to extend the warranty on a vehicle to include any augmentation to the vehicle bodywork. The only exception to this will be in the case of components supplied by the vehicle manufacturer and fitted by a manufacturer-approved contractor.

If components are fitted, the warranty on the panels to which they are attached is likely to be affected and probably cancelled. This is because the panels of the car will be subjected to loads for which they were not designed and the attachment of the extra components may damage any protective coatings on the vehicle.

Obviously this is important for the customers and they should be informed of any possible problems before work is started.

Your company may offer its own warranty to replace the vehicle manufacturer's warranty. This may be combined with a warranty from the manufacturer of the additional components.

A10.1.5 Customers are encouraged to ask questions and seek
clarification

Most customers will have a clear idea of the work they want doing and how they want the finished result to look. Once the work is done to the vehicle it will be a mobile showroom for your own company, so the customers must be happy with the finished result. If customers are pressured into making a decision, they may end up having work done that does not meet their original plans, or costs them more than they expected. If this is allowed to happen, you cannot expect them to be happy with the work carried out or to recommend you.

Always remember that the garage environment can be very unfriendly to customers. Because you work in a garage every day, do not be tempted to assume that your customers are as comfortable as you are with the surroundings. It is a good idea to show customers around the workshops and explain the work that is being done. This will probably generate a few questions that will help you understand the customers' concerns and answer them helpfully. Try not to use jargon and encourage the customers to ask if they do not understand the terms you are using. For example, show customers examples of what you mean by the different paint finishes available.

By taking your time with customers when the work is being discussed you can save a lot of time and trouble later.

If you suspect that the customer might not be clear on a point, it is always worth repeating the information in the form of a summary and asking, 'Do you understand?' or 'Are you sure?'. You should remember that you are not a pressurising sales person, but a professional giving advice. If the customer finds that he has bought the wrong item or modification he'll blame you.

A10.1.6   Where augmentation to vehicle bodywork would contravene legislation relating to vehicles, customers are given clear and accurate information about the implications of the contravention

There are strict laws governing the design of every vehicle on the roads in Britain and other European (EU) countries and these are designed to ensure the safety of passengers, other road users and pedestrians.

If a driver uses a vehicle that contravenes these laws he or she could be liable, so it is important that the customer is warned before any illegal modifications are made.

The are two areas to look out for when augmenting the bodywork of a vehicle:

Headlamp positioning. The headlamps on a vehicle may not be too close together or too high. This is to prevent them dazzling other drivers and to allow the lights to be directed and focused on to the correct position on the road to allow the driver a clear vision in the direction of travel.

Pedestrian safety. Vehicles must not have exposed sharp corners or objects that could pose an extra risk in the event of a collision. This is why vehicles no longer have mascots on top of the radiator grille (Mercedes and Rolls Royce have developed specially-hinged mascots, which will retract if involved in an impact, allowing them to comply with the law).

A10.1.7   Records relating to augmentation are complete and accurate and in the approved format

Make sure that you record all the relevant details of the job at every stage. This may be in the form of an estimate or quotation or authorisation from the customer. Get customers to sign their acceptance of the quotation so that there is no dispute after the work is done. These records may be part of your company's quality-control records.

A.10.2 AUGMENT VEHICLE BODYWORK TO MEET CUSTOMER SPECIFICATION

A10.2.1 *Appropriate protective clothing and coverings are used during augmentation activities*

Whenever you are working on a vehicle, it is essential that you wear the correct protective clothing. This means clean overalls and stout shoes (not trainers, since they offer little protection to the top of your feet). You must also have gloves, goggles and dust masks available for you to wear as required.

The vehicle you are working on needs to be protected, too. You should always use seat covers and some workshops cover the entire vehicle in plastic sheeting to keep it clean throughout the repairs (this can save time cleaning the vehicle after the repairs, too). Be particularly careful to protect the vehicle from welding sparks by using a fireproof mat or blanket. Overspray can be kept off by plastic sheeting or masking paper.

A10.2.2 *Appropriate information is accessed from appropriate sources to inform the augmentation of vehicle bodywork*

Before starting work, make sure that you fully understand what is to be done to the vehicle. Take time to read the quotation or work sheet. If you have any questions, ask the person who dealt with the customer. He will be able to help you, or contact the customer if there is any doubt.

The type of work involved in bodywork augmentation can be very varied and use many different parts or techniques. Read any instructions that accompany the components to be fitted, but do not hesitate to contact the manufacturer if you have any questions.

A10.2.3 *Components are fitted in accordance with vehicle/bodywork specifications using approved methods and equipment*

It is important to use the correct methods when you are fitting components to the vehicle. This means using techniques and equipment that are suitable for the type of components and the area of the vehicle where they are to be fitted. For example, it may be inappropriate to use rivets to attach components made of fibreglass which are more suited to being bonded in place using adhesives or sealers. The manufacturer of the components will specify the correct methods to be used.

If you fit **alloy wheels** to a vehicle you must ensure that you use the correct type of wheel nuts/bolts and that they are tightened to the correct torque setting. The torque setting should be checked after a short road test. Before driving the vehicle, check that the wheels do not foul on the body/chassis when the steering is turned on to full lock.

Motor cycle **luggage frames** and panniers are best fitted with chrome plated bolts as these both look good and resist corrosion.

When you are **joining cables** use the recommended type of connector. It is a good idea to solder joints were vibrations are likely to occur or a good electrical connection is essential. If you do solder joints you must use non-corrosive resin flux. Any new cables must be fitted so that they either fit into the existing wiring loom or can be run alongside using a proper loom wrapping. This is essential for car alarms so that they are not readily visible to the prospective car thief.

When **paint cover** is broken, such as by drilling a panel to fit a component, the paint edge should be re-sealed before the component is bolted into place. This will reduce the risk of corrosion around the area.

A10.2.4 Augmentation is completed in a manner which minimises risk of damage to other bodywork/components

It is very easy to rush into a job without taking the time to protect the areas of the vehicle that are adjacent to the area that you will be working in. This will leave vulnerable areas exposed. Every time that you offer up a part to check its fit, or apply adhesive to a panel, you risk damaging the surface of adjacent panels. It is well worth the trouble to cover the vulnerable areas with plastic sheeting or masking tape.

Remember to put tape on a surface before drilling any holes, as this will prevent the drill from skidding away from the target mark on to adjacent paintwork.

The key to carrying out the job quickly is to take the time to protect yourself from any accidents which could take valuable time and money to put right.

Some general points are: check that all the components will fit where you want them to go; before you drill a hole always check that there is nothing behind the panel, such as fuel or brake lines; when tightening bolts/nuts use the correct torque setting.

An example of checking where to fit components can be illustrated by looking at certain Ford Sierras fitted with rear spoilers. They had to be fitted with electrically-operated aerials which retracted automatically, because if you attempted to open the hatchback with the aerial extended the spoiler would snap the aerial off.

A10.2.5   Components and bodywork are adjusted to ensure correct operation

Once you have fitted all components you must check that all the affected doors, catches, switches and lights work correctly. This requires a methodical approach to make sure you have checked everything.

Pay particular attention to doors if sill extensions or replacement wings have been fitted. Side skirts are often fixed inside the door aperture and so they reduce the clearances. It is important to check that the doors close properly and do not foul the fitted parts.

If a front spoiler has been fitted you will need to check that all the affected lights and indicators still work correctly.

A10.2.6   Records relating to augmentation are complete and accurate and in the approved format

Make sure that you record all the relevant details of the job at every stage. This may be in the form of a job sheet that needs to be signed off once the work has been completed and checked to be satisfactory. These records may be part of your company's quality-control records, but they will also be a record that you have carried out the job correctly using all the correct parts and materials.

A10.2.7   Augmentation is completed to schedule in accordance with customer contract

Remember that the customer is having to make do without his car while the augmentation is carried out. Even if the customer has been supplied with a courtesy car, your company will want to have the courtesy car back as soon as possible, so it is important that the work does not take too long. Your company may well have undertaken to complete the work in a certain time and this may have been one of the reasons that they gained the work.

A10.2.8   Where augmentation is likely to exceed the agreed timescale, appropriate authority is informed promptly

There will always be problems that occur during work on a vehicle that were unforeseen and make it impossible to meet the schedule that has been agreed with the customer. If these problems are handled correctly they should not pose a serious problem, but you must let your supervisor know as soon as you encounter a significant difficulty that will require the schedule to be altered. This will give your company the chance to discuss the problem with the customer and agree a satisfactory solution. If the customer is not informed until the work is running late your company will have failed to meet the agreement it made with the customer.

A10.2.9 Augmentation activities are performed in accordance with statutory and organisational policy and procedure for health and safety

Your company will have rules that control what you may do in the workshop and how you are expected to act to look after your own health. Any workshop can be a dangerous place. We know a lot more than ever before about the harmful effects of the chemicals we use and the wide numbers of chemicals in use in a body repair workshop demand proper control and respect.

Your employer has a responsibility, under the Health and Safety at Work Act (1974) and the Control of Substances Hazardous to Health (COSHH) regulations, to look after your health and ensure that you know how to carry out the work safely, and it is in your own interest to follow the rules.

A12 UNDERPINNING KNOWLEDGE

MAINTAIN EFFECTIVE WORKING RELATIONSHIPS

A12.1 ESTABLISH AND DEVELOP PROFESSIONAL RELATIONSHIP WITH CUSTOMERS

Working in the motor industry involves working with people as well as working on vehicles. This means that you need to develop good relationships with both customers and work colleagues. In other words, you need to be able to get on with the people with whom you come into contact. This Unit is not about making friends. You may not like some of your customers or work colleagues, but you still need to speak to them and conduct professional or working relationships to get the job done. If you make an effort to work professionally with people they will respect you for that. You may also, over a period of time, develop friendships which last a lifetime. I have many friends and acquaintances whom I originally met as colleagues or customers.

A12.1.1 *Details sufficient for the needs of the developing relationships are established accurately and agreed*

No matter how good your company is at repairing vehicles, the success of the business depends on attracting customers and doing the job well so that they are happy to provide you with work. If you meet their needs well and give them confidence in the work that you are doing they will be more inclined to bring business to you in the future, and perhaps to recommend your services to their friends and colleagues.

Many companies spend most of their effort on developing the quality of their work and this can mean that they do not look at the rest of the service that they are providing. We are all very proud of the quality of our workmanship, and there is no doubt that the quality of the work that is done is a very important part of satisfying customers' needs. If the work that is done is not of a good enough quality, then you cannot expect the customer to be satisfied.

While every repairer boasts of the standard of his workmanship, many fail to recognise that the quality of work is probably not the only thing that the customer will be concerned about. No business can prosper without giving sufficient attention to the needs of its customers. Perhaps it is because most of our training is geared towards the quality of the repairs and doing a professional job that we can easily forget to think about everything else that the customer is looking for from a repairer.

After an accident the customer may be upset, angry, and harassed. In fact, every customer will have his own particular concerns and worries. If the work has been directed to your company by an insurance company, for example, it will be relying on you to look after the customer properly as part of the overall service that the insurance company provides.

Your job is to find out what the customer is looking for, so that you can then set about meeting those needs.

Because you spend your time dealing with repairs to vehicles, you are very familiar with the circumstances and the sight of damaged cars is routine. You are not usually aware of the background to the damage, or the circumstances of the accident. When you see a damaged car you are most likely to concentrate on the extent of the damage and the best way of repairing it.

A customer, who owns the car, will look on the damage in a different way. It is probably his own car, and the accident may well have been his own fault. It may be the first accident that he has had, and he certainly will not have enjoyed the experience! So, what is routine to you is in fact an upsetting and potentially expensive situation for your customer.

As an expert in vehicle repairs, the customer will be looking to you for advice, reassurance, and guidance. This will give you a good opportunity to talk to him and find out his concerns. Everyone who deals with customers who have had an accident in their car will be aware of the situation where a customer just wants to talk about the accident and tell you all about the circumstances. Instead of being bored by this (no matter how many times you may have heard a similar story before) you should try to listen carefully to the story to find out what the customer's concerns are. If you show an interest in his story, the customer will appreciate that you are concerned by his problems and that you are willing to treat his needs individually.

There are many common questions and concerns that may arise:
- How long will the repairs take?
- What effect will the repairs have upon the vehicle's warranty?
- Will you be able to match the colour of the paint?
- Can you carry out some extra work on the vehicle at the same time as the repairs?

- Will the car be safe after the repairs?
- Will the fact that the vehicle has been in an accident affect the resale value?

All of these types of question show you the things that the customer is converned about. Listen to them carefully, and note them down. If the customer is worried about how long the repairs take, you can show him how you can help and make sure that everyone involved in the repairs knows that it is important to repair the car quickly.

The customer who is worried about the quality of the work, safety, or warranty implications, can be shown some recently-completed jobs and perhaps be given a guided tour around the workshops if he is interested. This will show that you recognise his worries and are happy to answer them.

If the customer wants extra work done on the car, you will be only too pleased to discuss it with him, but you should be just as aware of the customer who is keen to keep the costs to a minimum. In both cases, you should talk to the customer carefully about the situation and how you are going to meet his concerns.

In many cases these discussions and agreements with customers will involve changing the specification of the repairs. This should only be done with the agreement of the customer and his full understanding. Many repairers will than ask the customer to sign the authorisation for the repairs to be carried out so that there is no doubt about what has been discussed and agreed. This may sound unnecessarily complicated, but experience will soon tell you that it is worth the effort.

By taking the time to understand the customers' needs and agree with them about the reapirs that will be done, you are not only ensuring that you satisfy their needs fully, but you are also preventing any potential problems once the reapirs have been completed.

If the customer comes to collect the vehicle after repairs and finds that the work does not meet what he expected, the situation can be very difficult and expensive to resolve. Importantly, too, it is very difficult to handle a situation like this without losing the customer's confidence. Once a customer has lost confidence in your compnay he will not want to come back, and you will have lost an important source of work.

Taking the trouble to investigate, recognise, and agree a customer's needs and concerns is part of providing a professional service, but it will also be a powerful tool in establishing a good reputation and keeping customers loyal and happy.

A12.1.2   Requests for information are responded to promptly and
information which meets customers' needs is presented
clearly, accurately and in a manner which promotes
customers' understanding

Customers may have questions that they need to ask at every stage of
your contact with them. The requests for information may come over the
telephone or in person, and may well be inconvenient for you to answer,
but they are always important to the customer and deserve to be answered
fully and helpfully. If the customer is given all the information that he
wants about his repairs he will have confidence in your service and a full
understanding of any difficulties involved.

If the replies to the queries are incomplete or late, they will lead the
customer to raise doubts about the repairs and lose confidence in your
company.

If the query is received by telephone, it may be helpful to record the call
on a form so that the query can be passed to the person responsible with
full details of when the call was received, the customer's telephone
numbers, and exactly what information is required. If the query is
received by letter it may be useful to stamp it with a date stamp so
that you know when the query was received. Using this kind of system
helps to make sure that the queries are answered quickly and efficiently.

When you are answering a query it is very tempting to give just the
briefest of details, or to use terms and information which the customer
may not understand. An explanation which may be clear to you and your
colleagues may not mean much to someone who does not know about the
repairs or the work involved. For example, if you tell a customer that the
car has 'just come off the Jig and is being DA'd ready for wet on wet', it
will not mean much. If you tell him that the chassis and body repairs have
been successfully finished and that the car is now being prepared for
painting, it will mean a lot more.

Similarly, to say that the repair will be completed 'some time next week'
may not be very useful to the customer. There may be very valid reasons
why you cannot be more exact about the expected day, but if the customer
does not know about these reasons he will be left with the impression that
the repairs are not being managed properly.

If you are able to give the customer full explanations for the situation
he will have more confidence in your abilities, and will not feel the need
to phone up frequently to make sure that his car has not been
forgotten.

A12.1.3 Customers are provided with sufficient accurate information to verify credibility

When you are communicating with your customers by letter, telephone, or face to face, they will be expecting you to show that you are fully aware of the repairs to their vehicle, that the vehicle is being repaired by professionals, and that the repairs are of a high quality and will be completed on time.

If a customer has doubts about the repairs he will have less confidence in the finished result, and will be less prepared to use your company in the future. These doubts can be raised even though you are answering queries accurately. For example, to tell a customer that the repairs will be completed on a certain day may seem to give the customer the information he wants, but the customer will be more able to believe what you are telling him if you are able to give him more information. Perhaps you could give information about the status and quick details of the work that still has to be done.

If the repairs have been delayed for some reason, it will not be enough to give simply a revised date for the estimated completion. The customer will want more information about what caused the delay and why you have been unable to work around it.

At the same time, remember that the customer could be easily worried if you give him the wrong kind of information. His confidence in you could be spoilt if you imply that you are having problems with the repairs. If there has been a problem with the repairs, or perhaps extra damage has been found, the customer could easily be alarmed if you let him think that this is giving you difficulties in carrying out the repairs. The information that you give should always be aimed to give the customer confidence in your abilities and reassurance that you are carrying out the repairs professionally and safely.

A12.1.4 Customers are treated in a manner which assists the development of a positive relationship

Good relations with your customers are very important to the success of your company. It is four times more expensive to gain a new customer than it is to keep an existing one, so no matter how much effort you put into advertising your business it will be wasted if you do not look after your existing customers. Every customer also has friends in the area and might possibly work for a company that has many cars of its own. This means that one pleased customer could prove a useful way of spreading your good reputation around the local area. Customers are particularly

187

inclined to listen to recommendations from friends when they are choosing which repairer to use, so by looking after your customers as well as you can you are also advertising your services to all their friends and colleagues.

It is the customers that enable your company to stay in business and prosper. This is why it is so important to treat customers well, and you should be aware of this every time you come into contact with them, whether it is in person, by letter, or on the telephone.

When the telephone rings, it should never be allowed to ring more than four times before it is answered. If you are busy with another customer, excuse yourself before answering the call, even if it is just to say hello to the caller and ask him to hold for a moment until you can talk to him properly. When you are talking on the telephone, try to be polite, clear, and helpful.

When a customer arrives, greet him with a smile and a cheerful welcome, no matter what you are doing. This will make him feel welcome and show that you are aware that he has arrived, even if you are busy dealing with something else at the time.

These kinds of gestures can take a lot of effort, and be difficult to remember when you are very busy, but they will make the customer feel welcome and appreciated. Be aware of this whenever you are the customer and you can pick up some good ideas, as well as examples of how not to treat customers. Listen to how other people sound when they answer the telephone, and learn from their mistakes. If you are treated well, think about what it was that made the difference and try to apply that to your own approach.

A12.1.5 *Where professional relationships with customers meet with difficulty, prompt appropriate assistance is sought*

No matter how hard you try, there may well be times when you are not able to look after a customer as well as he wants, or when you need help in dealing with a complaint. These situations are always possible, but what makes the difference is the way in which a company deals with them.

It is important that you know what to do if a customer has a complaint. Some companies record every complaint so that they can see what is causing them and take steps to stop them happening again. Recording a complaint can also help to make sure that it is resolved promptly and correctly by the right person. Your company may decide that all complaints should be dealt with by a senior manager. This will show the customer that his complaint is being taken seriously, even though somebody less senior could have dealt with the situation. Whatever the procedure is, be sure that you know what it is, so that when a difficulty occurs you are able to refer it to the correct person quickly.

If a customer is kept waiting, the problem will only be made worse, so everyone in the organisation should be prepared to help deal with the matter promptly.

A12.1.6 *Where information requests cannot be met immediately, prompt action is taken to meet these*

During a busy working day it may well not be possible to answer a customer's enquiry immediately. You may need to refer to a colleague who may be busy with another customer, or it may take time to find out the information from other companies such as parts suppliers. The danger is that if an immediate answer is not available the query can be forgotten.

If you cannot answer the query, let the customer know, explain the reasons politely, and let them know what you will do to find the answer for them. If there is a risk of the query being forgotten because you are busy, make a note of the query, and the customer's details.

If you have not been able to find an answer by the time you promised, it is worth considering contacting the customer anyway, even if it is just to let them know that you have not forgotten their request and that you are still waiting for the answer. This way the customer knows that you have remembered the query, and that you have not forgotten them.

A12.2 MAINTAIN WORKING RELATIONSHIPS WITH COLLEAGUES

A12.2.1 Colleagues are treated in a manner which promotes goodwill

Every day you will spend at least eight hours in the company of your colleagues, and you will rely on them to carry out other parts of the repair process to a suitable standard. It is therefore essential that you treat them in a way that encourages their confidence and creates a healthy working atmosphere.

It is a fact that we all work better when we are enjoying what we are doing. You have chosen to work with motor vehicles, and your colleagues will probably share your interest in them. Just like you, they will have a pride in their work, but they will also have the same concerns as you. They will be eager to produce high-quality work as efficiently as possible. You therefore already have a lot in common with them and many of your colleagues will go on to become close friends.

You company will need the repair process to run smoothly and this can only be achieved by everyone working in close cooperation with the other people involved in the repairs.

The simple rule is to treat everyone exactly as you would like to be treated. Even if you are having a bad day, try to be polite and friendly to everyone that you talk to, and remember that a happy working environment depends on everyone to cooperate. If someone asks to borrow a tool, or asks you to help them for a while, it is worth giving them the help that they need willingly. After all, it may be you that needs help from them tomorrow.

None of us likes to work with people who are unhappy or unhelpful, and you must always try to be aware of how much you are contributing to a happy, productive and enjoyable atmosphere in your workplace.

Of course, you cannot expect to get on in a friendly way with everybody. We cannot always choose the people that we have to work with, and inevitably there will be people that you find it difficult to cooperate with for any number of reasons. You must learn to cope with this situation, as it can arise frequently throughout your career. If there is a problem, don't be afraid to mention it to a supervisor, who will then be able to take this into account when allocating jobs or planning the workshop layout. The sooner you recognise the situation, the sooner you will be able to find ways to work around it so that it does not interfere with your work or the smooth operation of the workshop.

*A12.2.2   Reasonable requests from colleagues are met promptly and
          willingly*

Every vehicle that comes in for repairs will need teamwork for the repairs to be assessed, the parts ordered, the repair finished and the vehicle cleaned for delivery on time. Even the smallest job could involve several people, and it is essential that you all cooperate in getting the job done well and on time.

By working together closely, you and your colleagues will be able to help each other complete the repairs efficiently and perhaps boost your own wages as well as the customers' satisfaction.

If a colleague asks for your help, there is nothing to be gained from not giving your time. Of course it may not be convenient for you, and you may be involved in the middle of an important part of your work, but if the request is reasonable then do not hesitate to give your help. After all, it may be you that is doing the asking next time.

You will also have requests from colleagues to borrow your tools from time to time. Again, remember that it takes time to build up a comprehensive tool kit, and that so long as the tools are used properly, returned promptly, and not damaged you should be willing to lend them to others. You may want to borrow some of their tools one day, and helping them to get the job done is a way of helping the company as a whole. Your supervisors, too, will be expecting you to cooperate with other people.

*A12.2.3   When colleagues are meeting with work or personal
          difficulties, assistance is offered*

When you start work you will have to rely on other people to help you and offer you advice if you have a problem. As you gain more and more experience in your job you will be more able to help other people who work with you and offer advice to them if they want it.

Don't give advice if it is not asked for or if it is not welcome, but your colleagues should know that if they need help you are willing to cooperate if you can.

As your friendship with your colleagues grows, you will be able to help them in all kinds of ways. Personal problems can have a big effect on people and their approach to work, so if you can help with personal problems you will be helping to improve the work atmosphere at the same time. Again, never offer advice if it is not welcome, but as a colleague you should be approachable and prepared to help as much as you can. If you can take this approach you will build close and friendly working relationships that will make your working environment happy and hence productive.

A12.2.4 New colleagues are provided with information and support sufficient for their identified need

When you join a company there will be many new things that you need to learn. The company may have developed an induction process and checklist that is designed to make sure that new employees are told everything that they need to know. This will include safety procedures, rules, and introductions to important members of staff.

There will be lots of things that are not covered by this kind of induction, and this is where you and your colleagues can make a new member of staff feel welcome by taking the time to help them get acquainted with the business.

When a new colleague arrives, take the time to introduce yourself and make them feel welcome. If it is appropriate, introduce them to other members of staff, perhaps at rest breaks.

By helping them to get to know the company you will be helping them become a productive member of the staff.

It is in your interest to tell a new colleague about the area in which you work. This will save them making mistakes and will usually save time and trouble in the long term. Some of the points which you may need to make if you are involved in the induction of a new colleague are:
- names and titles of staff
- layout of workshop
- position of fire exits and fire extinguishers
- emergency evacuation procedure
- procedure for obtaining special tools and spare parts
- operation of hoists and other pieces of equipment
- company health and safety policy
- working hours and rest breaks

A12.2.5 Where a breakdown in working relationships cannot be resolved, prompt reporting action is taken with an appropriate authority

We cannot select the people that we have to work with, and inevitably there will be people that you find it difficult to cooperate with for any number of reasons. By being aware of this you should always try to be cooperative with all your colleagues even if you do not like them.

If there is a problem which you cannot ignore, or which starts to affect the smooth running of the business do not be afraid to mention it to a supervisor. The sooner you recognise the situation, the sooner you will be able to find ways to work around it. It is most important that this kind of problem is not allowed to affect the business.

Talk to your supervisors about the problem. The chances are that they will be aware of the situation and they will appreciate your responsibility towards the company as a whole. They may be able to suggest ways of solving the problem, or at least be able to take it into account when allocating jobs or planning the workshop layout.

A13 UNDERPINNING KNOWLEDGE

MAINTAIN THE HEALTH, SAFETY, AND SECURITY OF THE WORKING ENVIRONMENT

A.13.1. MAINTAIN THE HEALTH AND SAFETY OF THE INDIVIDUAL

A13.1.1   Guidelines, statutory regulations and safe systems for health and safety protection are followed

Every year over 2000 accidents in garages are reported to the local authorities and many more go unreported. Most accidents involve trips or falls, or poor methods of lifting or handling heavy items; serious injuries often result from these simple causes. Work on petrol tanks, in particular, causes serious burns, hundreds of fires and some deaths every year.

There are two main laws concerning health and safety in the workshop:

The **Health & Safety at Work Act 1974** requires anyone running a business to ensure, as far as is reasonably practicable, the health and safety of the people working in the business and anyone else who may be affected by what they do. The duties include people who:

- Work for the business, including part-time staff, trainees, and sub-contractors.
- Use the workplace.
- Are allowed to use equipment.
- Visit the premises (including customers).
- May be affected by your work (neighbours, the public, and other work people).

Everyone in a company has responsibilities under the Act, whether he is a manager or employee or self-employed. Everyone must co-operate with others in complying with the law.

The **Control of Substances Hazardous to Health** (COSHH) regulations 1988 set a legal framework for the control of hazardous substances for employers, employees, and the self-employed.

These regulations and others make requirements relating to most general premises including:

- All premises must be kept clean and rubbish and dirt must not be allowed to accumulate

- There must not be overcrowding: the number of people employed must not risk creating a danger to health.
- A reasonable temperature must be maintained, and a thermometer must be provided in a conspicuous place on each floor.
- The ventilation must be effective
- There must be sufficient lighting
- The toilets must be adequate and suitable and kept clean, and suitable washing facilities must be provided
- Floors, passages, steps and gangways must be soundly constructed and maintained and kept free from obstructions and slippery surfaces.
- Drinking water must be provided, and adequate eating facilities if meals are eaten on the premises.
- First aid provisions
- Fire provisions

There are also particular areas of concern in Body Repair that we will come to later.

The Health & Safety Executive (HSE) must be informed before new premises are occupied. The Health and Safety laws are enforced by the HSE or environmental health officers from the local council. They may come and inspect the business from time to time, particularly if there has been a complaint or an accident. The inspectors will be aware of the special risks of motor vehicle repair work, and they will be able to give advice on how to comply with the law. If there is a problem, they may issue a formal notice requiring improvements or, where serious danger occurs, they may stop the use of a process or equipment.

As a matter of routine, competent people such as insurance company engineering surveyors should carry out regular inspections of the premises. This will usually be done as part of the annual insurance renewal.

Of course, there are particular risks from the processes involved in vehicle refinishing. People employed as paint sprayers, or who work in the same premises, should be regularly examined as part of an on-going health surveillance process. In particular, this will involve lung function testing, which is a way of measuring the capacity and efficiency of the lungs. This test should be carried out at least once a year.

Every motor vehicle repair business employing five or more people must have a written policy for ensuring the health and safety of its staff. It should give the health and safety objectives of the business and clearly state how they will be met. By writing down the policy, employers are encouraged to decide their priorities and how they are going to meet legal requirements.

There are also certain documents that must be displayed. These include a copy of the employer's liability insurance certificate and large copies of certain employment laws.

When new employees join the company they should be given full instruction in the company health and safety rules as part of their induction into your working environment. This should be completed before they start any work. The items that should be included in this induction process are:

- Location of fire exits
- Assembly point in case of fire
- Location of fire extinguishers
- Location of eyewash
- Location of first aid point
- Name of trained first aider
- Rules for disposal of waste
- Rules regarding personal protective equipment
- Rules regarding respiratory protective equipment
- Other health rules; eg ear protection, smoking etc.

Once staff have been properly inducted, the responsibility for maintaining the safety of your workplace rests with everyone, not just your supervisors, and you should be constantly aware of your responsibility to yourself and your colleagues.

Once you are familiar with the safety policy you should observe it constantly and look out for any items that may present a risk. Always wear your safety equipment, and make sure that the equipment in the workshop is properly maintained and adjusted. In particular, keep an eye on electrical cables that may lie across the floor of the workshop and risk being damaged by feet or metal panels. Above all, keep the workplace clean and tidy and maintain high standards of housekeeping.

A13.1.2 Identified hazards in the immediate working environment are removed where possible

You must work in a safe manner or you are breaking the HSWA and are liable to a heavy fine and/or imprisonment. This means following the safe working practices which are normally used within the industry. The guidelines published by the Health and Safety Executive (HSE) and motor vehicle textbooks usually identify industry-accepted safe working practices. Examples of important procedures are:

- always use axle stands when a vehicle is jacked up
- always use an exhaust extractor when running an engine in the garage
- always wear overalls, safety boots and any other personal protective equipment (PPE) when it is needed, for example safety goggles when grinding or drilling and a breathing mask when working in dusty conditions
- always use the correct tools for the job.

Even if you are working in a safe and careful manner, you are still likely to spill the odd small amout of fluid or snag the air-line. This will then create a hazard. The procedure here is always to remove the hazard, no matter how it was created, immediately.

If you spill petrol or oil when you disconnect a pipe from the engine, you should clean it up immediately, or else you, or a colleague, may slip and fall. Absorbant granules should be used for this job, as they will soak up the liquid without causing a fire hazard or making the floor more slippery.

Brake fluid is a special hazard because if it is spilled on the vehicle's paint work it will soften the paint and may cause it to peel off, just like paint stripper. Therefore any spilled brake fluid should be wiped off immediately and the paint surface washed and polished if needed. Antifreeze spilled on paintwork will soften the paint surface and cause discoloration, so it too must be wiped off immediately with absorbant paper-roll/or towel and washed down if needed.

When working on any system which contains fluids, it is good practice to use a drip-tray to catch any possible spillages. This saves having to clean the floor as well as ensuring that all the used oils and fluids are disposed of safely. In particular, you can pour them from your drip-tray into your disposal container. The Environment Protection Act requires that you dispose of used oils and other fluids in a way which will not cause pollution. In practice, many vehicle manufacturers now collect used oil and brake fluid for re-cycling or to save employing other disposal procedures. Smaller garages without franchises will dispose of these liquids either through a private waste collection company or through a scheme operated in conjunction with the local authority. No waste oil, petrol, brakefuid or similar chemicals must be allowed to go into the drainage system.

All rubbish, such as used masking paper or plastic, should be cleaned up immediately and placed in bins. In the case of flammable waste these should be metal bins with lids so that there is no risk from fire. Many workshops have paper-baling equipment that compresses the waste into compact 'bales' that make better use of the space in bins and waste skips.

All paints and solvents should be kept in a ventilated space such as a paint mixing room. Fumes should be extracted at floor level as well as higher, since solvent fumes are often heavier than air.

Exhaust fumes are very dangerous; they can kill you. Small intakes of exhaust fumes will give you bad headaches, and over a time can cause lung and/or brain diseases. So ensure that you do not run a vehicle in a workshop without an exhaust extractor. Also ensure that the extractor pipe is correctly connected and is not leaking.

The airline used in most garages operates at between 100 and 150 psi (7 to 10 bar). This is a very high pressure, so it must be handled with great care. When you are using an airline always wear safety goggles to prevent dust entering your eyes. You must not use an airline for dusting off components, especially brake and clutch parts, as the very fine dust can cause damage to the throat and lungs. Before you use an airline ensure that the coupling is fitted firmly into the socket and that the pipe is not leaking anywhere along its length. Any damage or leaks should be immediately reported to your supervisor or manager so that they can be repaired. The high pressure of the air can quickly turn a small leak in an airline into a large gash, which in turn may make the airline whip around and cause damage to colleagues or to customers' vehicles.

Another area where you need to look out for damage is when using electrical equipment such as an electric drill, hand-lamp or grinder. Most mains-operated equipment runs at 240 volts and an electric shock from such a voltage could kill you straight away. Some companies use 110-volt equipment, which is operated through a transformer. This is much safer, especially if the transformer is fitted with an overload cutout. Handlamps should operate at 50 volts, or preferably 12 volts to give the highest level of safety. Plugs should only be fitted to electrical equipment by skilled persons; at the same time the correct amperage-rating fuse should be fitted and the equipment tested and logged in accordance with the Portable Appliance Testing Regulations (PAT testing). PAT-tested equipment should be numbered and carry a test-date label. Before you use any electrical equipment, visually check it for signs of damage and check that the cable is not frayed or split. Then ensure that you plug it into the correct voltage outlet. Do not attempt to use any electical equipment which you suspect may be faulty. Report the fault immediately to your supervisor.

*A13.1.3 Where identified hazards cannot be removed, appropriate
action is taken immediately to minimise risk to own and
others' health and safety*

There is a tremendous number of potential hazards in every vehicle
workshop. You will be using high-voltage welding equipment, vehicle
lifts, highly flammable paints, and hand-held grinders and saws. Even a
simple Stanley knife is a notoriously dangerous tool.

Most of these risks are an unavoidable part of the repair process, since
we cannot avoid having these items present in the workplace and using
them frequently. They will be safe if you are aware of the risks and
minimise them.

The company health and safety rules will require you to wear the
appropriate protective equipment and the importance of this cannot be
exaggerated. For your own protection you must have:

- Clean overalls, regularly changed (at least once a week)
- Goggles appropriate to the type of welding and grinding that you
  will be doing
- Gloves (thick PVC for use with rust and paint removers)
- Dust masks
- Suitable footwear
- Ear protection
- Breathing equipment for use in spray booths.

Some of this equipment will be provided by your company. We will
cover these areas more in section *13.1.7.*

There will always be power cables present in the workshop, but the
risks from trailing cables and air lines can be avoided by using overhead
power supplies. Many workshops now have supplies of electricity (13
amp and 3 phase) and compressed air combined into a unit suspended
above every work bay. This unit will probably also include dust
extraction facilities for connection with suitable tools.

Dust is an unavoidable product of the repair process, and it can cause
serious damage to your health over time. The risk can be largely avoided,
however, by using suitable dust masks and dust extraction equipment.
This sucks dust up rough holes in special abrasive papers and tools, and
carries it away to a large vacuum cleaner. This cleaner must be checked
regularly and emptied to ensure that the equipment stays effective.

Walkways and corridors, especially around fire exits, should be kept
clear of obstacles at all times.

A13.1.4 Dangerous situations are reported immediately and accurately to authorised persons

All hazards should be either removed or made safe. If you are aware of a hazard that is still dangerous you should report it immediately. This is your responsibility to yourself and to your colleagues.

Your supervisor, or the workshop manager, should be in a position to receive your report and act upon it. This is part of their responsibility and every employer has a duty to protect the health and safety of its employees.

However, if you are working alone or the matter is not a company one, then you must inform the relevant authority. The four main emergency services in the UK are Police, Fire, Ambulance and Coast Guard. To call them use any telephone and dial 999.

A13.1.5 Suppliers' and manufacturers' instructions relating to the safety and safe use of all equipment are followed

There are many items of equipment and machinery in the workshop that you will not have used before. If they are used correctly they should not present any hazard, but it is naturally important that you are aware of how they should be used. Do not take it for granted that your colleagues are using the equipment correctly. It is easy to get into bad habits when you are using equipment regularly, and many people do not take the trouble to learn about the equipment in the first place.

Some items of machinery, such as grinding wheels, are recognised as being particularly dangerous, and there are special signs that should be displayed near them to instruct you about the correct precautions that you should take.

Bottles of compressed gas also have regulations about how they should be transported and stored. Leaflets about this can be obtained from the gas supplier.

There are many other types of equipment that can be dangerous if they are not used properly, such as infra-red paint-drying equipment. Before you start to use them consult the instructions, and if you are in any doubt ask a supervisor. Using the equipment correctly will ensure that you are doing the job correctly and protecting your safety at the same time.

When using any hydraulic damage repair equipment or any vehicle-lifting equipment such as jacks, hoists or ramps, always observe the Safe Working Load (SWL). For example, many jacks and lifts may be rated at two tons, which is suitable for most private motor cars but may be close to the limit for larger panel vans such as Ford Transit, Renault Master,

VW Lts etc, where the unladen weight may be very close to or may even exceed the stated two-ton limit. If in doubt, check the vehicle's unladen weight which will be on a plate inside the vehicle, or ask your supervisor to check for you.

When using air-operated (pneumatic) tools and equipment never exceed the Safe Working Pressure (SWP) specified. When replacing grinding stones and abrasive discs always check that the maximum Revolutions Per Minute (RPM) of the abrasive disc is rated higher than the maximum RPM of the machine with which they are used. An abrasive disc which is under-rate for a machine may break up or fly off, causing major damage or injury to yourself or your colleagues.

A13.1.6 *Approved/safe methods and techniques are used when lifting and handling*

Repairing damaged vehicles can often involve lifting the whole vehicle, or removing and handling very heavy items such as engines and large body panels. It is important that when you carry out these tasks you use the correct techniques that avoid any unnecessary risks.

You should NEVER work underneath a vehicle unless it is safely supported, for example by axle stands.

At other times, you should always use a proper gantry or crane when handling engines or lowering a body on to chassis or subframes. Sometimes you will be spraying a vehicle with the engine or suspension removed, and in these cases it is essential that the vehicle is properly supported on stands.

You should never try to lift heavy items on your own, particularly if it involves stretching. It is easy to injure your back by using the wrong lifting techniques, so if in doubt ask a colleague to help you.

When you are lifting items from the floor always keep your back straight and bend your knees. Bending your back when lifting can cause back injury. If you keep your feet slightly apart, this will improve your balance. It is always a good idea to wear safety gloves when manually lifting. The maximum weight or load that you should lift is 20 kilograms, but as a trainee this may still be too heavy for you.

A13.1.7 *Required personal protective clothing and equipment is worn for designated activities in designated areas*

Again, the importance of personal protection in the workshop cannot be emphasised too much. Your health is too important to risk it by not taking the necessary precautions.

Your company rules will specify the items that must be worn during the different repair processes in designated areas.

Clean overalls should always be worn in the workshop. They will protect your skin from dust and chemicals as well as abrasion. Clean overalls also give a good impression to customers. If overalls get contaminated with solvents or very dirty they should be changed immediately, and a clean pair should always be available for you to use. Overalls should always be routinely changed at least once a week. Keep clean sets of overalls away from the workshop, and put soiled sets in a sealed bag

Goggles are absolutely essential for all welding and grinding work. Tinted goggles will be used for welding. NEVER weld without using goggles as the effect on your eyes could be permanent. It is sometimes possible to use a tinted screed that is attached to MIG welding equipment. During grinding, clear goggles will protect your eyes from hot sparks and dust. It is worth noting that there should be an eye-wash facility available.

Gloves should be worn as a matter of habit. When preparing or painting a vehicle the dusts and solvents that are used can cause a lot of damage to your skin, especially over time. Thin gloves will give you protection and you may choose to use barrier cream as well. If you are using rust removers or paint removers the gloves should be heavy PVC gauntlets

Dust masks should always be worn when you are using abrasives. Even if you are using dust extraction equipment, you should wear a mask as well.

Suitable footwear for the workshop will be stout shoes that will protect your feet from items falling on to them. They should also have thick soles to protect you if you stand on sharp objects. Trainers are not recommended.

Many people are unaware of the high levels of noise in a vehicle workshop. If you have to raise you voice to be heard you should consider using ear protection. This could be small ear plugs or ear defenders when using air chisels or hammers.

When you are applying coatings to a vehicle it is essential that you use breathing equipment. This will give you a clean supply of air and protect you from the high levels of hazardous chemicals that are present in spray booths. You should also wear disposable overalls.

You will often see safety notices requiring you to wear personal protective equipment (PPE) in some areas at all times. This is because other people are working in the area and you may be at risk. Hard hats are sometimes required when working under vehicles on a hoist.

A13.1.8 *Injuries involving individuals are reported immediately to competent first aiders and/or appropriate authorised persons and appropriate interim support is organised to minimise further injury*

Should there be an accident the first thing which you should do is call for help. Either contact your supervisor or a known first-aid person. Should either of these not be available, and it is felt appropriate, call for your local doctor or an ambulance.

You are not expected to be a first-aid expert, nor are you advised to attempt to give first aid unless you are properly qualified. However, as a professional in the motor industry you should be able to preserve the scene; that is, to prevent further injury and make the injured person comfortable. The following points are suggested as ones worth re-membering.

- switch off any vehicle or power source
- do not move the person if injury to the back or neck is suspected
- in the case of electric shock, turn off the electricity supply
- in the case of a gas leak, turn off the gas supply
- do not give the person any drink or food, especially alcohol, in case surgery is needed
- keep the person warm with a blanket or coat
- if a wound is bleeding heavily, apply pressure to the wound with a clean bandage to reduce the loss of blood
- if a limb has been trapped, use a jack to free the limb.

A13.1.9 *Visitors are alerted to potential hazards*

The best policy is not to let customers into the workshop. Many garages have a notice to this effect on the workshop door. For MOT purposes garages must have a customer viewing area. However, it is not always possible to keep people out of the workshop. Insurance company assessors and RAC/AA engineers will probably also require entry to the workshop, as well as some customers who are concerned about their vehicles. So, before allowing them into the workshop, you should warn them of potential hazards. For instance the dangers of oil and grease and the requirement to wear a hard-hat.

It is always a good idea to accompany customers when they are in the workshop. This way you can advise them if they look like they may do something potentially dangerous, or if there is a hazard of which they may not be readily aware.

A13.2 CONTRIBUTE TO THE LIMITATION OF DAMAGE TO PERSONS OR PROPERTY IN THE EVENT OF AN ACCIDENT OR EMERGENCY

A13.2.1 *Injuries resulting from accidents or emergencies are reported immediately to a competent first aider or appropriate authority*

Immediate and proper examination and treatment of injuries can reduce their effect and potentially may save a life. It is also essential to reduce pain and help injured people make a quick recovery. If you neglect an injury or give it insufficient attention it may lead to infection and ill health.

Every time that there is an injury, report it to your first aider and have the injury attended to. If necessary, they can arrange for treatment by a doctor or hospital.

A13.2.2 *Incidents and accidents are reported and recorded in an accident book*

Every company must have an accident book and all injuries, no matter how minor, should be recorded in the book. Some injuries and dangerous occurrences must also be reported to the Health and Safety Inspectorate. If the person is hospitalised for more than 24 hours or loses a limb the Inspectorate must be informed immediately on the telephone.

- The accident book will record:
- the name of the injured person
- the name of a witness
- the nature of the accident
- the treatment
- what has been done to prevent the injury happening again.
- date, time and place of accident.

A13.2.3 *Where there is a conflict over limitation of damage, priority is always given to the person's safety*

The safety of the injured person will always be of the utmost priority, and should never be compromised. Prompt, effective action at the early stages of an injury or accident will be essential if later treatment is going

205

to be effective. Do not worry about damaging clothing or equipment if there is a chance that your actions will help the injured person's safety.

Remember, in the event of an accident, people come first.

A13.2.4 *Professional emergency services are summoned immediately by authorised persons in the event of a fire/disaster*

An authorised person is somebody who has the task of carrying out a specific job. Anybody may call the emergency services if they are needed.

The four emergency services are:

Police

Fire

Ambulance

Coastguard

All are called by dialing **999** on an outside-line telephone. The emergency services' operator will ask you which service you require. In certain cases the police will automatically be called, for instance in the case of severe fires.

All emergency telephone calls are recorded on tape at the telephone exchange.

You will be asked for your name, the place where the emergency is and where you are calling from. With the introduction of electronic telephone exchanges the number which you are calling from is automatically recorded. You will be asked for the number to help confirm that your call is not a hoax.

Many companies have a direct telephone line to the fire station. These automatically call the fire service if a fire is detected by sensors or if the glass of a fire alarm is broken. In such cases, if the fire service is called out and there is not a fire, they may charge the company a large fee. So, do not tamper with such a device unless you are authorised to do so or there is a dangerous fire.

A13.2.5 *Alarm/alert/evacuation systems are activated immediately by authorised persons*

There will be fire alarm activation points throughout the workshops and the offices. Make sure you know where they are so that you can activate them quickly in the case of an emergency. Some of them may be linked automatically to the fire service, but they will all activate the alarm.

This will alert everyone in the building to the emergency, and start the routine evacuation of the buildings.

Do not worry about activating the alarm if you think that there is danger to people in the building. It is better to be cautious, and none of your colleagues will criticise you for taking their safety seriously.

When you hear the alarm, stop what you are doing and proceed immediately to the assembly area. Do not stop to collect personal belongings, and stay calm. At the assembly point a roll call will be taken.

You should have been made familiar with the evacuation procedures and the location of assembly areas during your induction.

A13.2.6 Selection of fire extinguishers is appropriate for a given type of fire

There are five different types of fire extinguishers in common use in garage premises. These are identified by their colour, as given in this table.

colour	type
red	water
cream	foam
green	vapourising liquid
blue	dry chemical powder
black	carbon dioxide

In addition there are 'fire buckets', full of sand, and 'fire blankets'.

Before you use any fire extinguisher you must ask yourself three questions:

1. Can the fire be put out easily?
2. If it cannot be put out easily can the spread of the fire be slowed down or stopped without risk by using an extinguisher?
3. Which fire extinguisher should be used?

To help you to choose the correct fire extinguisher, fires are classified into four classes.

class	description	colour of extinguisher
class A	fires of solid material, such as wood, paper, cloth, rubber	red
class B	fire of liquids such as petrol, paraffin, brake fluid	black, blue or green
class C	fire involving leaking gas such as acetylene, calor or natural gas	cream or blue

| class D | fires of metals which burn, such as magnesium and nickel. | blue, but it must be an inert dry powder. |

Liquid and gas fires are easily spread by using water, water can also conduct electricity.

Let us look at a few typical example of fires which sometimes occur in garages.

1. **Petrol spillage fire** - if this is on the forecourt the need is for quick action. The black carbon dioxide (CO_2) extinguisher will put out the fire and not leave a mark anywhere.

2. **Fire under the car bonnet**, cause unknown. Blue extinguisher using dry chemical powder is safe on both petrol and electrical fires. It is also easily cleaned off and will not damage the engine.

3. **Fire in a rubbish bin,** cause unknown. The use of a fire bucket full of sand or a fire blanket spread over the top of the bin should put out this fire.

Fires need fuel, oxygen from the air and heat. Remove any one and the fire will go out. Most fire extinguishers tend to both starve the fire of oxygen and lower the temperature of the fire so that it goes out.

A13.2.7 In the event of warnings, procedures for isolating machines and evacuating the premises are followed

When you hear an alarm sounding, you must stop what you are doing and leave the building calmly. Do not delay to collect belongings, but leave the workshop using the nearest fire exits.

For this reason it is important that fire exits, and passages leading to them, are kept clear of obstructions at all times.

The statutory notices displayed around the building will inform you of where you should go to have the roll call taken. This will be an assembly point identified by a green sign.

Machinery and equipment could be a threat to fire-fighters and other emergency services if it is not switched off and isolated from the electricity supply, as fire could damage the insulation around electrical cables. The paint store could also be a significant threat in a fire, so it should be secured and the fire doors should be firmly shut.

The precautions will normally be the responsibility of the workshop supervisor, and should be practised regularly as part of a fire drill. Make sure that you know what your responsibilities are and always follow them promptly.

A13.2.8 Reports/records are available to authorised persons and are complete and accurate

Records of fire drills are required to be kept by all companies with a fire certificate. They should state the date of the drill, as well as any problems that were encountered. The records should be signed by a manager.

The fire alarm system should also be checked regularly, and records of these checks should be kept for inspection.

The workshops may be inspected from time to time by the Fire Brigade, and these records will be inspected at the same time.

A13.3 MAINTAIN THE CLEANLINESS OF MACHINERY, EQUIPMENT AND WORK AREAS

A13.3.1 Machines and equipment are isolated, where appropriate, from the mains prior to cleaning and routine maintenance operations

Many items of equipment in the workship require routine maintenance and cleaning. This will make them safer to operate, and contribute to a healthier, more efficient workshiop.

Many items of equipment are electrical, and cleaning them with liquids could lead to a risk of electrocution. For this reason they should always be isolated from the electrical source before cleaning is started. In the case of hand tools it will probably be best to unplug them. Larger items of machinery may have a permanent connection to an electricity supply, with a large switch that can be used to disconnect the electricity.

If you are unsure about how the electricity should be disconnected, consult a supervisor. Never proceed if you are not confident about the correct method of isolating the mains supply.

When cleaning or carrying out routine maintenance on a machine, it is advisable go hang a 'DO NOT USE' sign on the main power supply box to ensure no one will switch the macine on by mistake.

Some tools use a supply of compressed air to power them, and this can generally be easily disconnected.

A13.3.2 Safe and approved methods for cleaning machines/equipment are used

There are three main items of cleaning equipment used in the garage. These are the cleaning bath (or tank), the pressure washer and the steam cleaner.

The cleaning bath uses a chemical solvent. This usually used for cleaning dirty/oily components. The components are submerged in the solvent and dirt is loosened with a stiff bristled brush.

The pressure washer is used for cleaning the mud off the underside of vehicles, using water at very high pressure will clean off mud. For hard-to-remove dirt, detergent can be added to the pressure washer.

The steam cleaner, often referred to as a steam jenny (jenny = generator), produces hot pressurised water with the option of detergent. This is used for removing very stubborn grease and dirt, like that found on the underside of high mileage goods vehicles.

If you are cleaning an engine or electrical equipment, it is important not to get water inside. Before cleaning inside an engine-bay with a pressure cleaner the electrical components and engine inlets should be covered with polythene.

When cleaning portable electrical appliances, be careful not to get water on the plug. This could cause a short circuit.

The mechanical parts of fixed machines may be cleaned with solvents, then dried with absorbent paper towel.

Never use compressed air to blow dust off equipment as it can be hazardous in the atmosphere; consider using a vacuum cleaner instead.

A13.3.3 Appropriate cleaning and sanitising agents are used according to manufacturers' instructions

Before using any solvent, detergent or sanitising agent such as bleach you must read the label on the container and read the COSHH sheet which the manufacturer or your company has prepared.

Solvent should only be used in the cleaning bath for which it is designed.

The pressure washer or steam jenny should only be used with the recommended detergent.

Electrical items can be cleaned with one of the many aerosol sprays which are available for this purpose, but the volatile fumes which are given off should not be breathed in at all.

You should remember that all cleaning agents should be kept away from your mouth and eyes and contact with your skin may cause irritation or a more serious skin malady. Always wash your hands and any other exposed areas of skin with toilet soap after carrying out a cleaning task.

A13.3.4 Used agents are safely disposed of according to local and statutory regulations

The Environmental Protection Act (EPA) and local by-laws in most areas require that used cleaning solvents must be disposed of safely. This means that they must be put into drums and either collected by a refuse disposal firm or taken to a local authority amenity site where they are put into a large tank for bulk incineration. Several local authorities, for instance Surrey and Hampshire, are now starting to look at ways of using the energy produced by burning waste material to produce electricity. Emptying used solvents into the drain can lead to a heavy fine or even imprisonment.

Detergents are by their nature biodegradable; that is, they break down and do not build up sludge like solvents, neither are they explosive like solvents. However, if you use large quantities of detergents, wash-bays which are fitted with the correct type of drainage system should be used.

A13.3.5 Machinery, equipment and work areas are cleaned according to locally-agreed schedules

Most equipment requires cleaning to prevent dirt and debris from building up around the operating parts. Dirt can cause excessive wear and heat build up, so regular cleaning is essential.

It may not be everyone's favourite job, but keeping your work area clean and looking after your equipment is all part of doing a professional job.

It is easy to overlook cleaning. If you are busy it will be difficult to find the time, so a routine for this kind of task is very helpful. Some larger companies employ cleaners so that their staff are free to continue with their work.

A13.3.6 Appropriate safety clothing and equipment is used when working with hazardous cleansing agents and equipment

To protect yourself from the cleaning agents which you are using you must, where appropriate, wear personal propective equipment (PPE). Most cleaning agents are poisonous and cause irritation or more serious complaints if allowed to come into contact with your eyes or skin.

Whenever you are working on a motor vehicle, it is expected that you wear cotton overalls and safety footwear. In addition the HSWA requires that employers provide and employees wear the appropriate PPE for hazardous jobs such as using cleaning equipment. The general requirements are as follows:

Cleaning Bath - rubber protective gloves, which extend over the user's wrists, goggles and plastic apron. Avoid getting solvent on your overalls as this can lead to skin irritation, be especially careful not to put solvent-soaked or oily rags in your overall pockets.

Pressure washer - rubber protective gloves and goggles, waterproof (plastic) over-trousers and jacket, and finally rubber boots (wellingtons). The idea is to be able to take the waterproof gear off and be dry underneath.

Steam cleaning plant - the hazard here is that, as well as being wet, the water is scalding hot. So the waterproof clothes must be of such a manufacture that they will protect the wearer from the high-temperature, high-pressure steam. That means thick and strong over trousers, coat, boots, gloves and a hat. A full-face mask is used to give complete protection.

GLOSSARY

AA	Automobile Association
ABS	Antilock Braking System
AF	Across The Flats (Hex Bolt Sizes)
'A' POST	Front door hinge pillar
BAR	Atmospheric pressure
CO_2	Carbon dioxide
COSHH	Control Of Substances Hazardous to Health
'C' POST	Rear door hinge pillar
DA	Dual Action
DOT	Department Of Transport
ECU	Electronic Control Unit
EFI	Electronic Fuel Injection
EPA	Environmental Protection Act
EU	European Union
GRP	Glass Reinforced Plastic
HGV (LGV)	Heavy Goods Vehicle (Large Goods Vehicle)
HSE	Health and Safety Executive
HSWA	Health and Safety at Work Act
LCS	Low Carbon Steel
MAGS	Metal Active Gas Shielded
MET	Mechanical, Electrical and Trim
MMA	Manual Metal Arc
MOT	Ministry Of Transport
OE	Original Equipment
PAT	Portable Appliance Testing
PC	Performance Criteria
PPE	Personal Protective Equipment
PSI	Pounds per Square Inch
PSV (PCV)	Public Service Vehicle (Passenger Carrying Vehicle)
PVC	Polyvinyl chloride
RAC	Royal Automobile Club
ROM	Read Only Memory
RPM	Revolutions Per Minute
SIPS	Side Impact Protection System
SWL	Safe Working Load
SWP	Safe Working Pressure
TAGS	Tungsten Active Gas Shielded

INDEX

215

mechanical/abrasive method
32-3
restoration of damaged surfaces
89
scheduling 52-3

bodywork augmentation
accurate descriptions 175-6
additional panels 175
adjusting components 181
alloy wheels 179-80
checking components 180
colour coding 175
contravention of legislation 178
  headlamp positioning 178
  pedestrian safety 178
covering vulnerable parts 180
disadvantages 176
  attachment of components 176
  late removal of components 176
  limitations to use of vehicle 176
exceeding timescale 181-2
information 174, 179
joining cables 180
luggage frames 180
methods and equipment 179-80
modified panels 175
paint cover 180
protective clothing 179
questions and clarification 177-8
record-keeping 178, 181
specialist finishes 175
statutory/organisational policy
182
warranty implications 177
within timescale 181

C

Car-O-Liner system 58, 62, 64-8,
72, 77-80

chassis frame re-alignment
equipment 104-6, 121, 124, 140
information 104
jig alignment fixtures 140
removal of damaged sections 136
  bolted joints 138, 141
  riveted joints 138, 141
  welded joints 136, 138, 142
restoration of surfaces 138-9
sealants 142
securing replacement sections
140-1
types of deformation
  diamond displacement 113,
  115, 120
  frame gauges 114-15
  local damage 114, 120
  sidesway 112, *113*, *116*
  twist 113, 114, 119
  vertical bends, humps, sags
  112-13, 115-16, 118
visual inspection 106, 111
work sequence and reinstatement
124-6, *127*, 142

cleanliness
machinery, equipment, work areas
  appropriate cleaning/sanitising
  agents 211
  disposal of materials 211-12
  isolation 210
  protective clothing/equipment
  212-13
  safe use of materials 211
  safe/approved methods 210-11
vehicle exterior
  according to customer
  expectations 146
  disposal of cleaning agents 147
  health and safety 147

216